A Corpus of Early Bronze Age Dagger Pommels
from Great Britain and Ireland

Ron Hardaker

British Archaeological Reports 3
1974

British Archaeological Reports

122, Banbury Road, Oxford OX2 7BP, England

General Editors:

    A.R.Hands, B.Sc., M.A., D.Phil.

    Mrs Y.M.Hands

    D.R.Walker, B.A.

Advisory Editors:

    C.B.Burgess, M.A.

    Neil Cossons, M.A., F.S.A., F.M.A.

    Professor B.W.Cunliffe, M.A., Ph.D., F.S.A.

    Sonia Chadwick Hawkes, B.A., M.A., F.S.A.

    Professor G.D.B.Jones, M.A., D.Phil., F.S.A.

    Frances Lynch, M.A., F.S.A.

    P.A.Mellars, M.A., Ph.D.

    P.A.Rahtz, M.A., F.S.A.

B.A.R. 3, 1974: "Dagger Pommels"   © Ron Hardaker, 1974

The author's moral rights under the 1988 UK Copyright,
Designs and Patents Act are hereby expressly asserted.

All rights reserved. No part of this work may be copied, reproduced, stored, sold, distributed, scanned, saved in any form of digital format or transmitted in any form digitally, without the written permission of the Publisher.

ISBN 9780904531022 paperback
ISBN 9781407320502 e-book
DOI https://doi.org/10.30861/9780904531022
A catalogue record for this book is available from the British Library
This book is available at www.barpublishing.com

DAGGER POMMELS

CONTENTS

	Page
LIST OF PLATES	
LIST OF TEXT FIGURES	
ACKNOWLEDGEMENTS	
INTRODUCTION	1
SECTION ONE	
The Typological Groupings	3
SECTION TWO	
The Corpus: Descriptions of the individual pommels	7
Index of Pommels	30
SECTION THREE	
The Associations	32
SECTION FOUR	
Postulated Chronology	39
SECTION FIVE	
Stylistic Affinities within the Corpus	45
GENERAL CONCLUSIONS	49
APPENDIX	52
BIBLIOGRAPHY	54
REFERENCES	57

LIST OF PLATES

		Page
Plate I a and b	Gold pommel mount from Topped Mountain, Co. Fermanagh (Corpus no. 28)	after 65
Plate II a - d	The gold pommel from Barrow 7, The Ridgeway, Dorset (Corpus no. 32)	
Plate II e	Amber pommel from Hammeldon Down, Devon (Corpus no. 33)	

LIST OF TEXT FIGURES

		Page
Fig. 1	1. The Ashgrove pommel (Corpus No. 1)	59
	2. The Amesbury pommel (Corpus No. 2)	
	4. The Milston pommel (Corpus No. 4)	
	5. The Garton Slack pommel (Corpus No. 5)	
Fig. 2	7. The Manton pommel (Corpus No. 7)	60
	8. The Galley Low pommel (Corpus No. 8)	
	9. The Narrowdale Hill pommel (Corpus No. 9)	
	16. The Winterbourne Stoke pommel (Corpus No. 16)	
Fig. 3	10. The Merddyn Gwyn pommel (Corpus No. 10)	61
	11. Bwlch y Rhiw pommel (Corpus No. 11)	
	12. The Wilmslow pommel (Corpus No. 12)	
	13. The Bedd Branwen (pot B) pommel (Corpus No. 13)	
	14. Bedd Branwen (pot H) pommel (Corpus No. 14)	
	15. The Marian Bach pommel (Corpus No. 15)	

Fig. 4	3. The Helperthorpe pommel (Corpus No. 3)	62
	6. The Gristhorpe pommel (Corpus No. 6)	
	17. Barrow 7, The Ridgeway pommel (Corpus No. 17)	
	18. The Eynsham pommel (Corpus No. 18)	
	19. The Garrowby Wold pommel (Corpus No. 19)	
	20. The Stanton Moor pommel (Corpus No. 20)	
Fig. 5	21. The Lockton Warren pommel (Corpus No. 21)	63
	22. The Scamridge pommel (Corpus No. 22)	
	23. The Winterbourne Stoke pommel (Corpus No. 23)	
	24. The Leicester pommel (Corpus No. 24)	
Fig. 6	25. The Skateraw pommel (Corpus No. 25)	64
	26. The Blackwaterfoot pommel (Corpus No. 26)	
	27. The Collessie pommel (Corpus No. 27)	
	28. The Topped Mt. pommel (Corpus No. 28)	
Fig. 7	29. The Shrewton pommel (Corpus No. 29)	65
	31. The Bush Barrow pommel (Corpus No. 31)	
	32. The Ridgeway Gold pommel (Corpus No. 32)	
	33. The Hammeldon Down pommel (Corpus No. 33)	
	34. The Grange pommel (Corpus No. 34)	

ACKNOWLEDGEMENTS

I am above all indebted to Mrs. F. M. Llewellyn who has at all times been a constant source of encouragement, advice and criticism. I would like to give her my thanks for kindly reading an earlier draft of the work and for allowing me to use her unpublished drawing of the Grange pommel.

I would like to express my gratitude to Miss A. S. Henshall for allowing me to make use of her drawings of the Scottish pommels and their daggers, and for her notes regarding the Leicester piece. Also to Dr. J. J. Taylor who kindly allowed me to publish her photographs of the Ridgeway gold pommel. I am grateful to the National Museum of Ireland for permission to publish Plates Ia and b, and to the British Museum for permission to publish Plate III.

I am grateful to the Archaeological Department of the University College of North Wales for affording me every facility possible in the production of this work, to Mr. R. G. Livens for providing moral support and to my friend and colleague Mr. R. B. White for many interesting and stimulating discussions.

Finally my many thanks to the curators and staff of the various museums visited for their generous assistance in allowing me to study the individual pieces, and to Mr. P. Brabner and Mr. J. Fisher for correcting my English.

INTRODUCTION

Generally speaking pommels had a three-fold purpose. Firstly to strengthen and cap the dagger hilt, supplementing the hilt rivets by providing an end-piece at the heel of the handle which united together the often complex hilt components. Secondly to balance the dagger, by providing behind the hand position a weight to counter-balance that of the blade and possibly create a comfortable and protected grip. Lastly, in addition to these functional purposes the pommel often allowed scope for the craftsman to show his ability in producing skilful decoration or simple decorative contrast by providing a decorated end-cap to the hilt, ultimately adding to the aesthetic qualities of the dagger.

Several of the pommels, particularly those which are better known, have been discussed by other writers, occasionally in some detail. However, all the pommels in Great Britain and Ireland have never been discussed either as individual types or taken as a whole, nor viewed in relation to one another. This monograph is an attempt as far as is at present possible to classify and collate a Corpus of Early Bronze Age dagger pommels in Great Britain and Ireland, and to discuss their typology, chronological relationship and cultural background.

The number of pommels known, or recorded as being at one time extant, is 34,[1] of which some have now been lost or destroyed, but records and drawings survive. This figure does not include a bone pommel noted by Evans[2] in the Kendal collection (now passed into the hands of York Museum) which has been lost, without record, nor the amber pommel destroyed during Cunnington's nineteenth century excavations at Winterbourne Stoke.[3] I have not included the Roke Down Dirk[4] with horn hilt and pommel, nor the possible bronze pommel (?) from Reach Fen, Cambridge,[5] since these pieces fall outside the chronological limits of the corpus.

In the term pommel, I have included the three Scottish gold pommel mounts and the gold mount from Topped Mountain Cairn in Ireland. Though not strictly speaking actual pommels, they nevertheless constitute a part of the hilt-end piece and provide an insight into pommel parts which have not survived.

SECTION ONE: THE TYPOLOGICAL GROUPINGS

Being closely related to the person the daggers and their pommels, like clothes, were subject to rapid changes in fashion and showed a variety of style, depending upon what was in vogue at the time of manufacture and on the taste and resources of the individual maker or owner. Consequently, in view of this fact and the small number of pommels known, very few of the pieces are exactly alike in style and dimensions or are associated with similar blades, which occasionally makes the typological classification of certain of the pommels a difficult matter. The pommels have been divided into typological groups according to common observed characteristics such as shape, size, and method of attachment and, in the case of the pommels of Group VI, the rather outstanding exotic or complex nature of the pieces has been considered reason enough for placing them in a separate miscellaneous category, even though they might possess certain characteristics found in the other groups.

Group I

It is possible to divide pommels made on the trough principle into two related, though distinct, varieties. This first group consists of pommels from Ashgrove (Fife), Amesbury and Milston (Wiltshire), Garton Slack, Helperthorpe and Gristhorpe (Yorkshire), and is characterized by their relatively straight sides, continuing the straight or slightly curving profile of their respective hilts, without the protruding upper lip of the pommels of Group II, which extends markedly beyond the hilt edge. Group I pommels are larger (see table, Appendix p. 52) and of more solid construction than the Group II pommels, and often appear oblong when viewed from above. They are in every case made from a single piece of material such as bone or horn, with a solid top and an opening or socket to accommodate a hilt-end tang cut into their lower edge. They are secured to the hilt-end by pins or rivets, the heads of which remain visible, driven through generally straightforward perforations at the front and back of the pommel.

Group II

This second group is made up also of trough pommels with mortised hilt-end receptacles and side pin perforations, and like the Group I pommels they are made from a single piece of material and have a solid top. The group comprises pommels from Galley Low (Derbyshire), Narrowdale Hill (Staffordshire), Merddyn Gwyn (Anglesey), Bwlch y Rhiw (Caernarvonshire), Wilmslow (Cheshire) and one pommel from the burial at Bedd Branwen (Anglesey). They are more rounded in profile and constitute a less marked continuation of the hilt edge, displaying a pronounced overhanging upper lip. They are much smaller and more fragile, being in every case under 35 mm. in length with correspondingly smaller and less regularly cut hilt-end receptacles.

Group IIa

Connected with the pommels of Group II are three pommels, which include a second piece from the Bedd Branwen burial, one from Cwm (Flintshire) and a pommel from Winterbourne Stoke (Wiltshire). They are closely allied to the Group II pieces in shape, size and hilt-end receptacle but differ in having in addition to the usual side pin perforations provision for pin attachment through the pommel top. These upper perforations might also be considered as transitional elements between pommels of Group II and Group III.

Group III

This group consists of four pommels, from the Ridgeway (Dorset), Eynsham (Oxfordshire), Stanton Moor (Derbyshire) and Garrowby Wold (Yorkshire), the first three displaying the protruding lip characteristic of Group II pommels, while the Garrowby Wold piece appears to maintain in its profile the edge of the hilt as evidenced by pommels of Group I. The pommels are characterized and differ from the trough types in that their tops are not solid but have an opening corresponding to that created by the extension of the mortised hilt-end receptacle through the pommel, probably for a decorative function.

Group IV

This group consists of four pommels which may be termed composite, since in each case the actual pommel is constructed from at least two components. The Lockton Warren and Scamridge (Yorkshire) pommels are made of three parts and appear to parallel certain features of the pommels of Group I, in particular the straight pommel sides appearing to continue the line of the hilt edge, and exhibit mortised receptacles, representing an alternative method of manufacturing a trough pommel. The Winterbourne Stoke (Wiltshire) and Leicester composite pieces appear more individual and display the straight sides of Group I. These composite pommels are relatively large in size as compared with most other pommels, for example the Winterbourne Stoke piece, when complete, must have been the largest pommel found in Britain.

Group V

Group V comprises the three similar gold pommel mounts from Scotland and a closely related mount from Ireland. These distinctive mounts were probably entirely decorative in function, consisting of thin strips or bands of gold. Their method of attachment and original position on the pommel or hilt is not known, and it is not clear what type of pommel was decorated with these mounts. The general size of the mounts and the original shape of the Collessie piece might suggest that they were attached to the necks of pommels affiliated to Group I.

Group VI

The final group is of a more miscellaneous nature, being made up of five disparate and for the most part unrelated pommels. This group in no way provides hard and fast typological limits, but is justified rather on the grounds of convenience and by the fact that the pommels are more complex, both in method of attachment where known, and in decoration where present.

This provides the criteria for their inclusion together as a miscellaneous group. Although reasonably comparable in shape, size, and structure to the pommels of Group I, the related pommels from Hammeldon Down (Devon) and Grange (Co. Roscommon) can be set apart from these types by their more complex method of hilt attachment and by the exotic nature of the Hammeldon Down piece. The Ridgeway gold pommel and the Bush Barrow (Wiltshire) pommel can also be seen to be of comparable dimensions to certain other pommels. However, because the nature of the pommels and their methods of hilt attachment are unknown, it is conceivable that they could be as close to the Hammeldon Down or Grange pieces as to the other types in respect of hilt attachment. In addition, their uniquely exotic qualities present a strong case for their being considered in this miscellaneous group of complex pommels. The rather complex pommel from Shrewton (Wiltshire) appears to be unique and without parallel among British pommels and has also been assigned to this group.

These typological groupings have been made on an empirical basis, dependent upon ordinarily observable features, without reference to other factors such as associations, circumstances and place of find, etc. At the moment too few pommels are known from British sites to make pommel typologies based on greater statistical analysis worthwhile. Unless more data becomes available it is unlikely that a more scientifically orientated assessment of the typological groups would be possible.

SECTION TWO: THE CORPUS

GROUP I

1. Bone pommel from Ashgrove, Methilhill, Fife
   (now in the Kirkcaldy Museum and Art Gallery)

   refs: Proceedings of the Society of Antiquaries of Scotland,
   XCVII (1963-4), 166-79.
   Henshall 1968, 182, fig. 41, 184

This pommel was found in a carefully made cist, situated near the sea, accompanying a crouched skeleton, probably of an adult male, a late coarsely made beaker showing roughly incised decoration, and a flat dagger blade with its three rivets still in place and showing traces of a sheath of animal skin. The pommel is one of the few known to have the remains of its original hilt surviving, it being constructed of two horn plates between which was probably a tanged third plate, now totally decayed, on to which the pommel was fitted.

The pommel (Fig. 1) is made from a single piece of ivory, almost certainly from the tooth of a sperm whale, which still retains in parts its original high gloss, though the lower edge has decayed away. It is 44 mm. in length by 16 mm. in depth, and has a rectangular, well mortised socket, and three pin-holes either side of the socket to accommodate the attachment pins, which have now disappeared suggesting they were of wood.

2. Bone pommel from Barrow 85, Boscombe Down, Amesbury, Wiltshire
   (now in Salisbury Museum)

   refs: Wiltshire Archaeological Magazine, LVI, 237-40.
   Moore & Rowlands 1972, 8, Appendix 38.
   Ashbee 1960, 100-102.

The pommel was found with an inhumation burial of an adult male which was primary to the barrow, accompanied by its flat dagger blade and a flint scraper. A secondary cremation burial from the same barrow produced a Bush Barrow type dagger and a small knife-dagger, neither of which have pommels surviving.

The pommel (Fig. 1) is made from a single piece of bone, and as it now exists is just under 40 mm. in length, and is badly decayed and out of shape. The method of attachment is not completely clear because of the lamination, but one can observe the internal hilt-end receptacle, though the lower sides of the pommel have decayed away and it is not possible to observe the side pin perforations. Three small metal pins survive which were probably used to attach the pommel to its yew handle, of which fragments remain, in the normal side pin manner. However, it might, by coincidence, be possible to observe three pin-holes in the pommel top, though this could not be properly ascertained because of the lamination, and in fact is most unlikely.

3. <u>Bone pommel from Helperthorpe, East Riding of Yorkshire</u>
   (now in the British Museum)

   refs: Greenwell and Rolleston 1877, 205-8.
   Evans 1881, 227, figs. 280-1.
   British Museum 1920, 83, fig. 77.

The pommel was found with its flat dagger blade near the centre of a barrow, accompanying a contracted inhumation burial of an adult male. The dagger appears to have been placed in the right hand of the deceased with the point of the blade touching the chin of the skeleton. It is recorded that the hilt was of ox horn, though little now remains, and was possibly composite in construction.[6]

This pommel (Fig. 4) is made from a single piece of horn, and appears to be in good condition, with a fairly well polished surface. It is 48 mm. in length, with a depth of 14 mm. and has a well mortised hilt-end receptacle, which suggests a sturdy dagger handle, the pommel being attached to the hilt by two side perforations.

4. <u>Bone pommel from Milston Grave 51, Wiltshire</u>
   (now in Devizes Museum)

   refs: Hoare 1810, 195.
   Evans 1881, 230-231, fig. 287.
   Ashbee 1960, 100-102.
   Annable and Simpson 1964, 41.

The pommel was found associated with a flat dagger of the multi-rivet type, accompanying a primary inhumation under a bowl barrow. The dagger hilt, judging by the present imitation, would have consisted of two separate wooden or bone plates, secured together by thirty small rivets which also had a decorative function. In addition to the rivets there is further hilt decoration in the form of dots incised into the hilt surface, forming firstly a border of double lines, but with only a single line around the heel of the blade, and secondly small circles between the rivets. This blade, along with that from Garton Slack and possibly that from Leicester are the only daggers with multi-rivet hilts which have pommels extant.

The pommel (Fig. 1) is constructed from a single piece of bone, now slightly restored, and is 44 mm. in length and 14 mm. in depth, though it is rather thinner than the other pommels of Group I. It has two side pin perforations, but it is not possible to observe the very probable hilt-end socket, since the nineteenth century imitation of the original handle has been permanently attached.

5. Bone pommel from Garton Slack, Barrow 107, East Riding of Yorkshire (now in Hull Museum)

refs: Mortimer 1905, 231-2.
Evans 1881, 228.

The pommel was found accompanying an inhumation burial of an adult male, which with several other burials was secondary to the barrow. The pommel was attached to a flat dagger with a multi-rivet hilt and was directly associated with an armlet. Also there appears to have been a food vessel associated with the group of secondary burials.

This is a very well preserved bone pommel (Fig. 1) slightly longer and wider and with a slightly more rounded profile than its Milston relation. It is made from a single piece of bone 49 mm. in length, with a depth of 14 mm., having a well mortised hilt-end receptacle, and two side pin perforations which are not placed on a horizontal line, one being lower than the other. The two pins survive and appear to be of bronze. The hilt, which does not survive, was probably of wood, and the pattern of the rivets suggests that it was very similar in design and appearance to the Milston hilt, differing only in the larger number of rivets (34 plus 4 for securing the hilt to the blade) and in the ornamental bronze strips delineating the curved profiles of the hilt and taking the place of the incised decoration in the Milston hilt.

6. <u>Bone pommel from Gristhorpe, near Scarborough, East Riding of Yorkshire</u> (now in Scarborough Museum)

   refs: Williamson 1872.
   Thurnham and Davis 1856, 152.
   Evans 1881, 228
   Ashbee 1960, 88-89.

The pommel was found with a contracted male skeleton buried in a large oak coffin placed at the foot of a grave pit beneath a barrow situated on a cliff overlooking the sea. The skeleton was originally wrapped in an animal skin fastened at the breast by a bone pin, and by its side was found a unique flat-bottomed dish made from pieces of bark stitched together and presumably containing a food offering. In addition the pommel was associated with a small flat dagger blade, and a small flint knife and flint scrapers were also present in the coffin.

Like the Ashgrove pommel (Corpus no. 1) which was similarly situated near the sea, the Gristhorpe piece is made from a single piece of whale bone and appears to be in almost perfect condition, still smooth and polished with a high gloss. It is very well constructed, with a very regularly cut hilt-end socket, and three side pin perforations, the pins for which no longer exist. It is the largest of this group of pommels, being 52 mm. in length with a neck depth of 20 mm., and in comparison with its accompanying small flat blade (Piggott Group I), appears inordinately large (Fig. 4). In fact the long survival tendency of the blade type, and its well used whetted appearance, compared with the almost perfect condition of the pommel, lead one to suggest that the pommel might not have been originally designed for the blade, but is a later substitution.

GROUP II

7. <u>Amber pommel from 'The Manton Barrow', Preshute Grave Ia, Wiltshire</u> (now in Devizes Museum)

   refs: Piggott 1938, 71
   Ashbee 1960, 75-6.
   Annable and Simpson 1964, 23-4, 47, 201.

This amber pommel was found with its small, flat knife-dagger beneath a bowl barrow, accompanying a primary inhumation burial of an adult female, the skeleton being wrapped in cloth before consignment to the grave. Also associated with the burial were a grape cup, a pointillé decorated incense bowl, three bronze awls, a gold bound amber disc, a halberd pendant with its bronze blade set in a haft of sheet gold, and an assortment of beads and buttons, while nine feet away from the skeleton was a small cinerary urn apparently used as a food vessel. The value of the amber pommel and the richness and variety of these grave goods suggest that the owner was a woman of wealth and rank.

This is a very small pommel (Fig. 2) made from a single piece of amber, 22 mm. in length with a depth of 10 mm. The amber appears cracked and fragile and slightly decayed at the top. It has a small mortised socket and two pin-hole perforations either side, the pins for which do not appear to exist. Unlike the Gristhorpe pommel it appears to be correctly proportioned in size to its small blade, suggesting that the pommel was originally designed for the blade.

8. Bone pommel from Galley Low, Brassington Moor, Derbyshire
(now in Sheffield Museum)

refs: Howarth 1899, 54, 115-16.
Bateman 1848, 39.

The pommel was found in a barrow containing several inhumations, and was probably interred with an adult skeleton. A small collared urn, a small flint arrowhead and a bone pin with a large perforated eye were also in probable association with the burial. The excavation revealed no evidence of either a dagger blade or a hilt.

The pommel (Fig. 2) is made from a single piece of bone, 32.5 mm. in length, and with a depth of less than 10 mm. It appears, like most of this group, fragile, and is slightly chipped and pitted on one side, but elsewhere appears smooth and polished. The pommel has a small mortised hilt receptacle, which is rather irregular, varying in thickness from one end of the pommel to the other. Three ribs have been left along the base of the receptacle, as though the maker believed the hollowing out to be too difficult for the fragile pommel, or that there was no necessity for precision tooling.

There are three side pin-hole perforations, though no pins appear to have survived.

9. Bone pommel from Narrowdale Hill, Alstonfield, Staffordshire
   (now in Sheffield Museum)

refs: Bateman 1848, 97-8.
      Howarth 1899, 94-5, 181.

The pommel was found in a small cist placed a little to one side of the central cist under a small low barrow. The cist contained a cremation burial, originally protected by a large urn, but this has not survived. Also found with the pommel, amongst the cremated remains were a flint arrow head and a piece of stag's horn.

This pommel (Fig. 2) is more rounded in shape, appearing almost like a button or a stud (which is what the excavator originally believed it to be). It is made from a single piece of bone 19.5 mm. in length and with a neck of 12 mm., and has the small, pronounced overhanging lip found in the other pommels of this group, though it is smaller than them. It appears to be remarkably well preserved, with a smooth well-polished surface, and has a small, well-defined, almost circular, hilt-end receptacle. The three side pin-hole perforations are somewhat unusually placed, two being placed close together in the centre of the pommel side near the base of the neck, while the third is high up to one side. The three corresponding holes on the other side are not exactly analogous as the middle two holes run into each other, while the corresponding side hole is lower. This suggests that the holes were bored from the one side, and after crossing the socket the boring process was not kept in perfect alignment.

10. Bone pommel from Merddyn Gwyn, Pentraeth, Anglesey
   (now lost)

refs: Hughes 1908, 211-20.
      Lynch 1970, 150, fig. 52, 151.

The pommel, without hilt or blade, was found amongst the cremated bones of a woman, inside an enlarged food vessel. This was one of four later burials secondary to a beaker inhumation in the barrow which had been enlarged to accommodate these subsequent burials.

The pommel (Fig. 3) is made from a single piece of bone of which only one half remains, the break occurring along the length of the pommel, giving it a similar broken shape to that of the pommel from Bwlch y Rhiw (Corpus no. 11). It is 33 mm. in length with a depth of 10 mm. to the base of the neck. It has two side pin perforations and a probable oval hilt-end socket. The damage to the pommel suggests that it might have been burnt, but this is not stated in the excavation report.

11. Bone pommel from Bwlch y Rhiw, Caernarvonshire
(now in the National Museum of Wales, Cardiff)

ref: R.C.A.M. (Caerns) 1964, XXXVIII, fig. 10, XXXIX.

The pommel is listed in the inventory of the Royal Commission without mention of either hilt, blade or attachment pins, simply noting that the pommel was found with a cremation in an urn together with a bronze awl, the burial being protected by a stone cist.

This is a fragile pommel (Fig. 3) made from a single piece of bone of which only one half survives similar to the piece from Merddyn Gwyn (Corpus no. 10), probably as a result of burning. It is 27 mm. in length with a depth of 9 mm., and has a tiny hilt-end socket and two small pin-hole perforations.

12. Bone pommel from Wilmslow, Cheshire
(now lost)

ref: Evans 1881, 228, fig. 283.

The pommel was found without evidence of blade or hilt, accompanying a cremation burial contained in an urn.

The pommel (Fig. 3) is made of a single piece of bone 35 mm. in length by 1 mm. in depth, with a more pronounced overhanging lip and proportionately longer neck than the others of the group. The small mortised receptacle has been made by drilling three holes side by side in the underside of the neck, slightly overlapping them to form a continuous cavity. This would suggest that attachment to the hilt-end tang was either difficult or inexact. Two small side pin perforations are present, but no pins survive.

13. Bone pommel from Bedd Branwen, Llanbabo, Anglesey
(now in Bangor Museum)

refs: Lynch 1970, 133, fig. 44.
Lynch 1971, 31, 32, 61-3.

The pommel was found without evidence of dagger blade, pins or hilt inside a large collared urn which contained the cremated bones of an adult male. The mouth of the urn had been blocked by a piece of earth and a sandstone hone on which the non-existent blade could be sharpened. This pommel from pot B was among the secondary series of cremation burials, the primary series producing a pommel of group IIa (Corpus no. 14).

The pommel (Fig. 3) is constructed from a single piece of bone, is 35 mm. in length and with a neck depth of 10 mm. It exists in its complete form, though slightly cracked and chipped as a result of the cremation. It has a fairly narrow, well defined, mortised receptacle and two proportionately large side pin-hole perforations.

GROUP IIa

14. Bone pommel from Bedd Branwen, Llanbabo, Anglesey
(now in Bangor Museum)

refs: Lynch 1970, 128, fig. 42.
Lynch 1971, 31, 32, 61-3.

The pommel from the primary series of burials in the barrow, was found amongst the cremated bones of an adult male, which were placed under an inverted urn (pot H) and protected by a stone cist. Associated with the pommel were a simple polished bone bead, six amber beads, and four carved jet beads.

The pommel (Fig. 3) is made from a single piece of bone, slightly smaller than the other related Group II pommel (Corpus no. 13) in the burial mound, being 30 mm. in length and 5 mm. in depth. Like other pommels from Merddyn Gwyn and Rhiw (Corpus nos. 10 and 11), only half of the piece now exists, being split longitudinally probably as a result of the cremation and of the weakening of the pommel by the hilt-end socket. This socket appears to be small, and in addition to one side pin perforation the pommel exhibits in its flat top one definite pin-hole near the outer edge, and what appear to be two pin-holes placed on the centre line. The other half of the pommel is missing, but there was presumably a fourth hole near the opposite edge. The four top pins would have been vertically attached to the hilt-end tang, supplementing the one horizontally attached side pin.

15. Bone pommel from Marian Bach, Cwm, Flintshire
(now in the National Museum of Wales)

ref: unpublished.

The pommel was found under a round cairn, accompanying a secondary cremation burial contained in a large collared urn. There were no other associations.

The pommel (Fig. 3) is made from a single piece of bone of tiny proportions, being 28.5 mm. in length with a depth of 5 mm. It has a small hilt-end socket and two side pin-hole perforations placed close together. The pommel top is not solid, a proportionately large elongated hole being present, perhaps as a result of a pin-hole perforation in the centre of the pommel top which enlarged itself along the point of greatest weakness. It is also possible that a hilt-end tang was intended to extend through the pommel as has been suggested for the open-ended pommels of Group III, though the very small size and the varying alignment of the upper hole with the lower part of the hilt-end socket indicate that this is unlikely. The hole might even have been caused by an error of workmanship in the construction of the socket, or alternatively it might be due to damage during the cremation.

16. Bone pommel from Winterbourne Stoke, Grave 66, Wiltshire
(now in Devizes Museum)

refs: Hoare 1810, 114, pl. XIII.
Annable and Simpson 1964, 65, 121.

The pommel was found associated with a bronze knife-dagger, accompanying a primary cremation placed in a collared urn, and buried beneath a bowl barrow. Also found in the urn were some 'black beads' which are now lost.

The pommel (Fig. 2) is made from a single piece of bone 34 mm. in length with a depth of 10 mm. and is comparable with Group II pommels in shape and size. The pommel is well preserved and has a well made hilt-end socket. It is unusual in its method of pin attachment, having five side pin perforations on one side, the other incorporating six holes, as two holes at the upper left end of the pommel run into each other - suggesting one hole had been drilled too high and a lower, correcting hole was drilled into it. The pommel top has in addition two perforations probably for pins set vertically into the hilt-end tang.

GROUP III

17. Bone pommel from Barrow 7, The Ridgeway, Dorchester, Dorset
(now in Dorchester Museum)

refs: Proceedings of the Dorset Natural History and Archaeology Society, 1936, LVIII, 20.
Thomas 1965-66, 4.

The pommel was found with a three-riveted dagger blade,[7] accompanying a secondary inhumation burial in a barrow containing three other burials, the latest of which produced the well known gold pommel (Corpus no. 28). A stone mace head and a flint axe were also found in association with the pommel.

The pommel (Fig. 4) is well preserved, appearing fairly smoothly polished, only slightly chipped and rather finely constructed from a single piece of bone. It is 32.5 mm. in length with a depth of 13.5 mm. and is very similar in shape to the pommels of Group II, with a pronounced overhanging lip. The pommel has two fairly large side pin-hole perforations and a well defined mortised hilt-end receptacle, which extends through the pommel, creating in the centre of the pommel top a rectangular opening 16 mm. by 6 mm. in size. This opening would have been filled by the projecting top of the hilt-end tang, which might have been in the form of a knob or other decorative shape extending beyond the pommel end. More probably it was finished flush with the pommel, creating an attractive contrast of white bone pommel surrounding the probably darker wooden inlay of the hilt-end tang. The pommel shows slight traces of burning, which is puzzling as it is associated with an inhumation burial.

18. Bone pommel from Foxley Farm, Eynsham, Oxford
(now in the Ashmolean Museum, Oxford)

refs: Thomas 1965-66, p.4.
Inventaria 1956, G.B. 14.

The pommel was found with its dagger blade accompanying a tightly contracted skeleton of an adult male buried in a grave, one of a cemetery of eighteen grave pits. The small bronze dagger blade was flat and possessed three rivets.[8] Also present with the burial was a beaker, classified by Clarke as belonging to his F.P. type.

The pommel (Fig. 4) is made from a single piece of bone and appears fairly well preserved. It measures 35 mm. in length by 14 mm. in depth, and appears to be almost exactly similar to the Dorchester pommel (Corpus no. 17). The Eynsham piece has two side pin perforations and a hilt-end socket which extends through the body of the pommel to form a rectangular opening in the centre of the pommel top. The end piece of the hilt no doubt created a decorative inlay in the upper surface of the pommel, in a similar manner to that of the Dorchester piece.

19. Bone pommel from Garrowby Wold, Barrow 32, East Riding of Yorkshire
(now in Hull Museum)

refs: Evans 1881, 228.
Mortimer 1905, 146, fig. 391.

The pommel was found with its dagger blade accompanying the contracted skeleton of an adult male, buried under a barrow. The bronze dagger blade is flat, possesses three rivets and appears heavily whetted. The excavator recorded that the almost completely decayed remains of a horn handle were also found.

The pommel (Fig. 4) is made from a single piece of bone, 44 mm. in length with a neck 12 mm. in depth, and is fairly well preserved. Unlike the Dorchester and Eynsham pommels, it does not have a pronounced lip, is less rounded, and has a top in the shape of an elongated oval. The piece has two side pin-hole perforations, while the hilt-end socket is extended uniformly through the pommel, creating a large oval opening 38 mm. in length by 5 mm. wide which is practically the same size as the socket opening in the lower side of the pommel. The opening would have been filled by the top of the hilt-end tang, probably finished flush with the pommel top.

20. Bone pommel from Stanton Moor, Birchover, Derbyshire
   (now is Sheffield Museum)

ref: Derbyshire Archaeological Journal, 1936, 21-42.

The pommel was found in a small stone box-cist, apparently without a covering barrow, accompanying the cremated bones of a young woman. Associated with the pommel were a riveted bronze dagger blade now very incomplete and distorted, exhibiting what appears to be a decorated central rib, a perforated bone pin, a bronze pin and three flint scrapers, all contained with the cremated remains in a now fragmentary cinerary urn.

This pommel (Fig. 4), made from a single piece of bone, appears to be in almost perfect condition and is the most complex and unusual of the pommels of this group. In profile it has affinities with Group II pommels in having an overhanging lip. When viewed from above the pommel top appears almost circular, 34 mm. in diameter, with a corresponding circular hilt-end socket continuing through the pommel, widening to 20 mm. in diameter at the top, giving the pommel the appearance of a bone ring. The pommel has a small neck, less than 10 mm. in depth, and has an unusually complex pin arrangement, with a total of four pin-holes, placed at an equal interval around the pommel ring. When viewed from the top the first and second quadrant pin-holes are normal side perforations, running horizontally through into the hilt-end socket, while the third and fourth holes are placed in the underpart of the overhanging lip and run upwards at an angle into the inner edge of the pommel top. This angle of alignment might suggest that the hilt-end tang extended a little way out from the pommel top, or that there was a separate end-plug probably in the shape of a domed cap, slightly wider than the pommel opening to enable the pins to penetrate into the tang. However, both these possibilities seem unlikely as the angled pin-holes are not diametrically opposite one another and all existing pommels appear to have had flat tops without such extensions.

GROUP IV

21. <u>Bone pommel from Lockton Warren, Walkingdon, near Pickering, Yorkshire</u>
    (now in York Museum)

    ref: unpublished.

The pommel and dagger were originally in the Mitchelson private museum at Pickering, and were possibly found by Thomas Kendall during his explorations of many of the barrows around Pickering. Since Kendall regrettably kept no notes of his diggings, and the manuscript catalogue of the Mitchelson collection has long been lost, nothing is now known of the finding of the piece or of its associations other than the dagger blade. The flat, triangular shaped dagger blade is probably made of bronze and is attached to the hilt by means of three rivets.

The composite pommel (Fig. 5) is made of three separate bone parts, and has a length of 50 mm. and a depth of 21 mm. The pommel is in a bad state of preservation, the middle and one of the outer pieces hardly surviving, and as a result of this decay, coupled with the nineteenth century hilt restoration, it is impossible to ascertain properly the inner composition of the pommel. It appears to resemble the Scamridge pommel (Corpus no. 22) with its middle component providing the receptacle by a rectangular cut in its lower edge, the two outer pieces acting as sides to the socket. The pommel has a rather straight profile, similar to that of pommels in Group I.

The pommel has three side pin perforations, the upper two still containing what appear to be the original bronze pins, while the centrally placed lower one has no pin surviving. The upper two pins do not pass through the socket and its tang, but simply hold the plates together, only the centre pin serving to attach the pommel to the hilt-end tang.

22. <u>Bone pommel from Scamridge, near Pickering, Yorkshire</u>
    (now in Sheffield Museum)

    refs: Bateman 1861, 225-6
    Evans 1881, 228
    Howarth 1899, 75

The pommel was associated with a single extended inhumation burial under a barrow. It was accompanied by its now fragmentary flat bronze dagger blade, which appears tongue shaped and probably possessed three hilt attachment rivets, and also by several bone and flint scrapers.

This is a particularly fine bone pommel (Fig. 5) and apart from a small break is almost perfectly preserved, still retaining its original smooth, polished surface. It is 52 mm. in length, with a depth of 18 mm. and is very similar in profile to the pommels of Group I. The pommel consists of three parts: its centre piece, having a centrally placed receptacle cut from its lower side, forms the hilt-end socket with the two outer pieces. It has four side pin perforations, the upper two still retaining their original pins which serve to rivet the pommel components together, while the two centrally placed perforations (without pins surviving) attached the pommel to the hilt-end tang. The missing pins might possibly have been made of wood or other perishable substance.

23. Bone pommel from Grave 4, Winterbourne Stoke, Wiltshire
(now in Devizes Museum)

refs: Hoare 1810, 122, pl. XIV.
Annable and Simpson 1964, 48, 102.
Thomas 1965-66, 4-6.

The pommel was found with a Camerton-Snowshill type dagger,[9] accompanying a primary cremation placed in a wooden coffin under a large bell barrow with a pond barrow impinging upon its ditch on the south side. The surface of the dagger still bears traces of a leather sheath and pointillé ornament can be seen on the upper part of the mid-rib. The pommel was also associated with a small bronze knife-dagger with its pommel missing, a pair of bone tweezers and two fragments of sheet bronze.

This pommel (Fig. 4) now exists as two almost perfectly preserved pieces of highly polished bone, 34 mm. in length by 13 mm. in depth, each exhibiting an overhanging lip. The two are diagonally opposite quadrants and each is perforated by two side pin-holes which still contain the original bronze pins. It seems likely that their inner corners would have touched, dividing the pommel into four equal quadrants. The two alternate quadrants of the pommel, since they do not survive, could well have been made of wood which no doubt became dark through use, affording an attractive contrast with the alternate bone pieces, providing a cruciform pattern. Whether the wooden inlays were part of the handle as has been suggested or were attached with the bone mounts to a central hilt plate cannot be ascertained, as nothing remains of the hilt.[10]

24. Ivory pommel from Leicester
(now in Leicester Museum)

ref: Evans 1881, 230-1.

This pommel was found with an inhumation burial in a grave near Leicester city centre. There was no evidence of a covering mound. The pommel was associated with a dagger blade of the multi-rivet hilt type, evidenced by the nine hilt-attachment rivets at the butt of the flat blade, the rivets for which do not appear to have been found.

This composite pommel (Fig. 4) consists of two pieces of ivory, each with a slightly overhanging lip. Its outer side is 45 mm. in length and 14 mm. in depth. They are separated by a bronze plate of similar shape to the pommel which appears to extend through from the top of the pommel, from which it emerges as a bronze tang 27 mm. wide, extending now to a length of just over 20 mm. Bored through this bronze plate are three rows of rivet holes, the upper two containing three rivet holes, the lower as a result of damage containing only two (the rivets for these still surviving). It seems likely that this bronze plate acted as a centre plate, extending through the hilt from the pommel to the blade.[11] In addition to its functional use, the plate would have provided an attractive bronze inlay visible from the top and sides of the pommel and also the sides of the hilt. There also appears to be some decorative milling along the upper edge of the plate in the pommel top. The two ivory pieces are pinned to the bronze plate by two small, widely spaced bronze pins.

GROUP V

25. Gold pommel mount from Skateraw, East Lothian, Scotland
(now in the National Museum of Antiquities of Scotland)

refs: Childe 1946, 119, 121.
Henshall 1968, 183, 185, fig. 42.

The pommel was found placed with its dagger at the side of an inhumed skeleton, buried inside a stone cist under an 'immense cairn' constructed near the sea. The flat bronze dagger blade with two rivets shows an unusual tang at its heel and it is possible that the uniform layer of corrosion covering the blade might suggest that it was incorporated into a sheath.

This is the best preserved of the four pommel mounts of this group (Fig. 6) and is made of a sheet of gold decorated by four ribs divided by three grooves. This gold strip has been cut into two pieces and as a result is slightly distorted, now appearing perhaps more circular than in its original form, which might have been a somewhat pointed oval about 38 mm. in length, probably similar in size to the corresponding collar-piece of the Ridgeway gold pommel. It is slightly tapering in profile with its outer surface apparently worn smooth, while along the top and bottom edges the gold strip is turned in as flanges which appear unworn with roughly cut inner edges.

26. Gold pommel from Blackwaterfoot, Arran, Scotland
(now in the National Museum of Antiquities of Scotland)

refs: Proceedings of the Society of Antiquaries of Scotland 1901-2, XXXVI, 120.
Proceedings of the Society of Antiquaries of Scotland 1922-3, LVII, 129, 131.
Henshall 1968, 183, 185, fig. 42.

The robbing of a very large cairn exposed a well made cist which was completely empty except for the pommel and its dagger blade. The accompanying bronze blade is flat except for three delicate ribs or lines of punched dots, and shows two rivets with an unusual angular tang at the heel of the blade.

This pommel mount (Fig. 6) is similar to that from Skateraw (Corpus no. 25), appearing as a narrow strip of sheet gold which is now in two pieces and greatly distorted, measuring 5 mm. in width with a probable length of about 41 mm. though it is difficult to estimate the original shape and size. The sides of the mount are decorated with six ribs divided by five grooves, and it has rough edged flanges similar to those of the Skateraw piece.

27. Gold pommel mount from Gask Hill, Collessie, Fife
(now in the National Museum of Antiquities of Scotland)

refs: Proceedings of the Society of Antiquaries of Scotland, XII (1876-8), 451-3.
Proceedings of the Society of Antiquaries of Scotland, LVII (1922-3), 129, 131.
Henshall 1968, 186.

The pommel was found beneath a large cairn accompanying a cremation burial in a cist, which was secondary to an inhumation associated with a beaker. Also present among the cremated bones was a flat, three-riveted bronze dagger blade showing the remains of a sheath of wood and animal hair.

This pommel mount (Fig. 6) is made of a strip of sheet gold almost identical to that from Blackwaterfoot (Corpus no. 26), and is now greatly distorted and broken into two. At the time of its discovery it was intact and oblong in plan, with rounded ends, measuring approximately 30 mm. along its length. It has a depth of 7 mm. and is decorated in exactly the same manner as the Blackwaterfoot mount, displaying six ridges separated by five grooves, and with similar flanged edges.

28. Gold pommel mount from Topped Mountain, Co. Fermanagh, Ireland
(now in the National Museum of Ireland)

refs: Harbison 1968, 51.
Harbison 1969, 37.

The pommel was found with its dagger blade, accompanying a primary inhumation burial in a cist. Also present in the cist were a food vessel and a secondary cremation burial. The associated bronze dagger blade is decorated by three grooves on each face, which follow the outline of the blade, which appears to have been attached to the hilt by three rivets.[14]

The gold pommel mount (Plate I a, b; fig. 6) is in the shape of a strip constructed from a single piece of gold foil, the surviving portion measuring approximately 31.5 mm. in length by 6 mm. in width. It appears slightly distorted and corroded, and is decorated by four central raised ribs separated by three grooves, while the edges of the mount are marked by a regular notched decoration. The hilt and pommel, like those of the Scottish mounts, do not survive. This suggests that they might have been of some perishable material such as wood.

29. Bone pommel from Barrow 5K, Nett Down, Shrewton, Wiltshire
    (now in Salisbury Museum)

   refs: Case 1966, 157.
         Moore and Rowlands 1972, 8, 10, fig. 1.

The pommel was found with its flat bronze dagger blade accompanying a crouched inhumation burial at the foot of an oval shaft hewn into solid chalk. The crouched skeleton was grasping a beaker of Clarke's Developed Northern Group, while at the entrance to the shaft there was another inhumation burial with a later beaker type. The blade possesses a flanged tang containing two vertically placed hilt attachment rivets, and appears to have been wrapped in moss and placed inside a bag of woven fabric before consignment to the grave.

This unique and complex pommel (Fig. 7) is constructed from a single piece of bone and displays a curving top 40 mm. in length, which protrudes as an overhanging lip from a narrow neck, the neck extending into a projecting tenon over 20 mm. in length. This projecting neck, which contains in each side four pin-hole perforations, three upper and one lower, is hollow and acts as a receptacle for the hilt-end tang. It is likely that the hilt, of which nothing remains, was composite, its hilt plates probably having been attached to the outside of the pommel tenon, while the centre plate entered the hollow tenon in the form of a tang with final securing attachment provided by the pins. The piece was probably a most difficult article to manufacture and fit on to the hilt.

30. Bone pommel from Standlow, Derbyshire
    (formerly in British Museum, now lost)

   ref: unpublished

This bone pommel was in the British Museum but is at present lost, and no records appear to be available except for a short note in the British Museum's accessions register, which reads: "bronze dagger blade, with one rivet remaining and a bone (pommel) end of the handle. Length of bone 1 inch". It appears to have been a tanged and riveted dagger found with a stone battle-axe. The tiny sketch in the register shows the pommel apparently as similar to the Shrewton piece (Corpus no. 29) and to that from Leicester (Corpus no. 24), but the drawing does not allow further distinction to be made.

31. Pommel from Bush Barrow Grave 5, Normanton, Wiltshire
(fragments now in Devizes Museum)

refs: Thurnham 1870, 454.
     Evans 1881, 232.
     Piggott 1938, 62
     Ashbee 1960, 76-8.
     Annable and Simpson 1964, 22-3, 99.
     Moore and Rowlands 1972, 10.

The fragmentary remains of the pommel were found with the probably extended inhumation of an adult male under a huge bowl barrow. The value of the pommel pieces is equalled by the richness of the accompanying grave goods, which include a grooved, six-riveted dagger blade manufactured from almost pure copper (for which it is likely the pommel pieces formed the hilt-end), a slightly larger grooved six-riveted blade of bronze,[13] a small bronze knife-dagger (neither of the latter blades appearing to have pommel or hilt surviving), a gold belt hook, two lozenge-shaped sheets of gold with incised decoration, a polished stone mace head, bone mounts and a flanged copper axe, all of which suggest a high degree of wealth and social standing in the owner. Cloth impressions were visible on the face of the axe, while adhering to the copper blade belonging to the pommel were the wooden and leather fragments of a sheath.

Unfortunately little remains of either the haft or the pommel but nine small fragments which survive indicate that they were both made of wood decorated with an inlay of minute gold pins 10.6 mm. in length, which were driven in flush with the surface of the wood. These several thousand gold pins were in no way functional but appear to have been strictly decorative. Judging by the surviving fragments and a drawing made at the time of its discovery and published by Thurnham, the pommel appears to have been completely decorated with gold pins, the lower part having the pins arranged in a chevron pattern above which was an additional arrow patterned inlay created by the same kind of fine gold work. (Fig. 7). The heel of the haft was similarly decorated with the gold pins, but without the pattern arrangements, while the central portion of the wooden hilt remained undecorated, affording an attractive contrast of plain wood between the decoration of the hilt base and the pommel. It is difficult to ascertain whether there was a separate pommel, and if there was, whether it was composite or of one piece, since no pommel attachment pins were found and the remaining fragments do not indicate either pin-holes or separate pommel components, or a hilt-end receptacle. It is also difficult to ascertain the exact size of the pommel, though it is likely that it was large, being probably over 60 mm. in length, with a depth of about 20 mm., creating with its large copper blade a very impressive weapon.

32. The Gold Pommel from Barrow 7, The Ridgeway, Dorset
(now in Dorchester Museum)

refs: Drew and Piggott 1936
Grinsell 1959, 141
Ashbee 1960, 101-2, fig. 30
Taylor 1970, 216-221

The pommel was found with a cremation burial lying eighteen inches below the top of the mound of a large bowl barrow, which contained in addition a primary inhumation without grave goods, a secondary inhumation which produced pommel Corpus no. 17, one other secondary cremation, and several scattered finds. The pommel was directly associated with two bronze dagger blades of Bush Barrow type,[12] one of which is assumed to have provided the blade for the pommel. Also found in direct association was a small knife-dagger (without a pommel) and a slightly flanged bronze axe.

This pommel (Plate II a - d; fig. 7) is large, 55 mm. in length with a depth of 19 mm., and displays a flat, oval shaped top and a slightly overhanging lip. It is made of sheet gold providing an end-cap for a hilt made probably of wood which has not survived, and which may have been only roughly finished in the area to be covered by the pommel.

To construct the pommel the smith probably pre-formed the cap from a single piece of gold, and hammered a single strip of gold into a band for the collar. The hilt-end was apparently coated with pitch, traces of which remain inside the pommel collar, the combination of pitch and pins providing the maximum adhesive strength and the greatest finish. The decoration consists of concentric grooves around the lower edge of the collar and the upper face of the cap in addition to an inner oval of five grooves which conform to the shape of the pommel, while lateral chevrons are found evenly spaced around the edge of the cap. The decoration was probably left until the pitch had hardened slightly and was probably made with a bone or wooden stylus which left a tapering rounded groove. The pitch would have provided a good working surface permitting a clean, deep decorative impression as can be seen by the sharpness of the grooved lines on the inside. The pommel originally held thirtytwo pins, of which seven survive, three of which are still held precisely in place by the pitch. These pins, which were entirely functional, are approximately 1.2 mm. in length by 0.47 mm. in diameter and were hammered in flush with the gold foil about 1 mm. below the upper edge of the pommel collar.

33. Amber pommel from Hammeldon Down, Devon
(no longer extant)

refs: Evans 1881, 228-9, fig. 284
Kendrick 1937, 313
Ashbee 1960, 101

The pommel was found accompanying a cremation, the only burial under a round barrow. The piece was also associated with a badly preserved bronze dagger blade, which appears to possess a slight mid-rib and grooved lines on each face corresponding to the outline of the blade.[15]

This remarkably beautiful pommel, unfortunately destroyed during a Second World War air raid on Plymouth, was constructed from a single block of red amber, being approximately 60 mm. across the top by 43 mm. wide, with a neck of 14 mm., the pommel seeming slightly large in proportion to its now fragmentary blade.

The pommel (Plate IIe, fig. 7), has a flat, highly polished top, with a slightly overhanging lip and a rounded collar below which the mount tapers to a small oval platform. It is decorated with small inlaid gold pins formed by drilling tiny holes about 2 mm. deep into the amber and tapping down into each a short length of gold wire, which was then cut off flush with the surface. These decorative gold pins are found around the lip of the pommel top, the lower edge of the pommel collar, and on the top surface, the latter in a cruciform pattern. Corresponding with the ends of this cruciform shape, four decorative bands of pins descend to the lip of the lower platform, around which is a single row of pins, while the lip, cruciform and underside lines are delineated by three rows of pins. Certain of these additional rows of gold pins either appear to be afterthoughts or were not hammered with the same care or precision. On the pommel lip in particular the middle pins often appear to be irregularly placed and occasionally encroach on to one another. The method of attachment is complex: a central tenon projects from the pommel base, retaining along its two lateral sides a small mortised receptacle. The pommel tenon would have entered a socket in the dagger hilt, and would have been attached to it by means of only two pins evidenced by the two small pin-holes drilled through the tenon, while the mortised receptacles in the pommel would have accommodated possibly hilt plates or more likely hilt-end projections. In addition to their functional effectiveness the pommel tenon and receptacles were designed so that no attachment pins would be visible on the exterior surface of the pommel, as the hilt plates would hide the two tenon pins. Such was the value of the pommel that a small piece of amber which had broken off was replaced, possibly by the original craftsman, and attached by means of horizontal pegging, and secured firmly in place by seven additional gold pins, exactly similar in style and form to those used in the original inlaid decoration. Though the amber piece has again been severed along the original weakness, the repair pins still remain around the fracture.

34. Bone pommel from Grange, Co. Roscommon, Ireland
(now in the National Museum of Ireland)

refs: Harbison 1968, 51
Harbison 1969, 10

The pommel was found under a large barrow with a secondary cremation burial (grave 10), which was protected by an inverted cordoned urn, while the burial primary to the mound contained a globular pygmy cup and two food vessels. Also associated with the pommel was a rolled-up, grooved six-riveted dagger.[16]

This pommel (Fig. 7) is made from a single piece of bone, now slightly decayed and chipped probably as a result of the cremation burial. It is 45 mm. in length and with a depth of 15 mm., having a flat oval top, a slight lip and gently curving sides. The method of attachment appears to represent a more complex version of the trough principle, as a narrow tenon projects from the floor of the pommel trough to the base of the pommel, creating two mortised receptacles, which would probably have accommodated a double hilt-end tang. The pommel tenon would have entered a corresponding socket in the hilt-end, while the pin attachment is by means of two alternate diagonal perforations drilled through the tenon, the pins presumably being driven through the hilt-end tangs before the hilt plates were added. The pinning must have been a difficult affair, as the tenon perforations would have been obscured by the hilt-end tangs. Two small indentations are visible, one in the upper corners of each of the pommel receptacles, caused probably by the original drilling of the diagonal pin-holes or less probably by the actual pinning process. This method of attachment, like that of the Hammeldon Down pommel, is designed so that no attachment pins would be visible on the outer surface of the pommel.

INDEX OF POMMELS

The pommels and their locations	Corpus No.	Page
Alstonfield, Staffs - see Narrowdale Hill		
Amesbury, Wilts - see Boscombe Down		
Ashgrove, Methilhill, Fife	1	7
Bedd Branwen, Llanbabo, Anglesey	13 & 14	14
Birchover, Derbyshire - see Stanton Moor		
Blackwaterfoot, Arran	26	22
Boscombe Down, Barrow 85, Amesbury, Wilts	2	7
Brassington Moor, Derbyshire - see Galley Low		
Brigmilston, Wilts - see Milston		
Bush Barrow, Grave 5, Normanton, Wilts	31	25
Bwlch y Rhiw, Caerns	11	13
Collessie, Fife - see Gask Hill		
Cwm, Flints - see Marian Bach		
Dunbar, East Lothian - see Skateraw		
Foxley Farm, Eynsham, Oxford	18	17
Galley Low, Brassington Moor, Derbyshire	8	11
Garrowby Wold, Barrow 32, Yorks	19	17
Garton Slack, Barrow 107, Yorks	5	9
Gask Hill, Collessie, Fife	27	23
Grange, Co. Roscommon	34	28
Gristhorpe, near Scarborough, Yorks	6	10
Hammeldon Down	33	27
Helperthorpe, Yorks	3	8
Leicester	24	21
Llanbabo, Anglesey - see Bedd Branwen		
Lockton Warren, Yorks	21	19
Manton Barrow the, Preshute, Grave 1a, Wilts	7	10
Marian Bach, Cwm, Flints	15	15
Merddyn Gwyn, Pentraeth, Anglesey	10	12
Methilhill, Fife - see Ashgrove		
Milston, Grave 51, Wilts	4	8
Narrowdale Hill, Alstonfield, Staffs	9	12
Nett Down, Barrow 5k, Shrewton, Wilts	29	24
Normanton, Wilts - see Bush Barrow		
Pentraeth, Anglesey - see Merddyn Gwyn		
Preshute, Wilts - see Manton Barrow		
Ridgeway the, Barrow 7, Dorset	17	16
Ridgeway Gold Pommel the, Barrow 7, Dorset	32	26
Scamridge, near Pickering, Yorks	22	19
Shrewton, Wilts - see Nett Down		
Skateraw, East Lothian	25	21
Standlow, Derbyshire	30	24
Stanton Moor, Birchover, Derbyshire	20	18
Topped Mountain, Co. Fermanagh	28	23
Wilmslow, Cheshire	12	13
Wilsford, Grave 5, Wilts - see Bush Barrow		

INDEX OF POMMELS continued

The pommels and their locations continued	Corpus No.	Page
Winterbourne Stoke, Grave 4, Wilts	23	20
Winterbourne Stoke, Grave 66, Wilts	16	15

SECTION THREE: THE ASSOCIATIONS

The objects associated with each pommel have already been briefly mentioned with the descriptions of the individual pommels in the Corpus, for greater ease of reference. These notes are further supplemented by the Appendix (p. 52), consisting of tabulated association lists which make for a fuller comparison and help to clarify the discussions in this chapter.

Group I

The pommels of Group I were found in every case with inhumation burials, all of which appear to be primary to their barrows with the exception of that from Garton Slack (Corpus no. 5). All of the pommels are found with their dagger blades present, which in every case are of Piggott's flat groupings[17] and are made of bronze, without blade decoration or grooved outlines. With the exception of the Milston (Corpus no. 4) and Garton Slack (Corpus no. 5) daggers, which have multi-rivet hilts, the blades show either two or three rivet hilt attachments and very in size. The blade accompanying the Amesbury pommel (Corpus no. 2) has been analysed[18] and shows a fairly high tin content with a certain amount of arsenic. The piece is further interesting in that a secondary cremation burial in the same barrow produced a Bush Barrow type dagger classified by Gerloff as type Ic, possibly with its pommel deliberately broken off,[19] and a small knife-dagger also without a pommel. The Milston (Corpus no. 4) and Helperthorpe (Corpus no. 3) pommels appear to have no other associations apart from the blade. The blade associated with the latter piece has the appearance of being well worn through use and repeated whetting, which suggests a functional rather than an ornamental use of the piece. The pommel from Garton Slack (Corpus no. 5) was found in association with what is most likely an armlet, consisting of a narrow strip of sheet copper or bronze which is decorated and flanked by two hooked wire strands. This

32

armlet appears to be closely related to bracelets such as that from Knipton, and its multi-strand arrangement brings it in line with analogous examples from the later phase of the Reinecke A. The only pottery associations are a coarse biconical beaker, found accompanying the Ashgrove piece (Corpus no. 1) which has been classified by Clarke as S4, thus appearing late in his series, and a questionable association of a food vessel with the Garton Slack pommel.

Group II

Of the seven trough pommels comprising this group, the pommel from the Manton Barrow (Corpus no. 7) is conspicuous for its association with a rich series of grave goods, including a small, flat bronze knife-dagger. These grave goods, consisting of a plain incense cup, a grape cup with sixteen perforations, a gold-bound amber disc, various exotic beads, a halberd pendant with a bronze blade set in a haft of sheet gold and three bronze awls, testify to the wealth and importance of the deceased. None of the other pommels in the group possesses a comparable assemblage of exotic associations and in addition no other pommel in the group has been found with a blade or has produced evidence of a blade surviving, which is significant. In fact the only metal found associated with the other pommels was a small bronze awl of just over one inch in length found with the pommel from Bwlch y Rhiw (Corpus no. 11). In funeral rite the general trend of the group is to cremation burial, only the Manton and Galley Low pommels being from inhumations. All of the pommels were found accompanying pottery, and excepting the pommel from Merddyn Gwyn (Corpus no. 10) were associated with cinerary urns. The Bedd Branwen (Corpus no. 13), Galley Low (Corpus no. 8) and Bwlch y Rhiw pommels, along with that from the 'Manton Barrow' were found with collared urns, though the last might not have been in direct association with the urn. The Narrowdale Hill pommel (Corpus no. 9) was found under a very large, undecorated coarse urn and was associated with a smaller, neatly decorated cordoned urn. The Merddyn Gwyn pommel is recorded as accompanying an enlarged food vessel with well defined shoulder stops, but which appears similar to other local cinerary urns found in Anglesey.

Group IIa

These three pommels, like the great majority of those of group II, are from cremation burials contained in a cinerary vessel, in each case of the collared urn type. The Winterbourne Stoke pommel (Corpus no. 16) differs in that, unlike the Welsh pieces, it was found with a small knife-dagger which exhibits three rivet holes and slight mid-rib markings.

Group III

Of the group of open-ended pommels, those from the Ridgeway (Corpus no. 17), Eynsham (Corpus no. 18) and Garrowby Wold (Corpus no. 19) were from inhumation burials, while the Stanton Moor piece (Corpus no. 20) was found in a cremation burial. All of these pommels are each associated with a bronze dagger blade, those from Eynsham and Garrowby Wold are of the three rivet flat variety, both being included by Piggott in his flat dagger series. The blade associated with the Ridgeway pommel has three rivets and has been included by ApSimon in his group of blades 'derived from or related to Bush Barrow types'.[20] It is noteworthy that the pommel and blade appear stratigraphically earlier in the barrow than the gold pommel (Corpus no. 32) associated with two apparently typologically early Bush Barrow type daggers.[21] The Stanton Moor pommel was found associated with a riveted bronze dagger blade, which possibly exhibits a decorated central rib suggesting it might be typologically late. The only pottery associated with the group is a now fragmentary and consequently typologically indistinguishable urn found with the Stanton Moor pommel and a beaker accompanying the Eynsham piece. This beaker has been classified by Clarke as FP, which presumably is equivalent to S3 and therefore late in his series, Clarke's late classification being supported by Lanting and van der Waals, who place the beaker in their final stage of the development of beaker types in the Wessex region.[22]

Group IV

Of the four composite pommels those from Leicester (Corpus no. 24) and Scamridge (Corpus no. 22) were associated with inhumation burials, while that from Winterbourne Stoke (Corpus no. 23) was found with a cremation (the associated burial of the Lockton Warren pommel is not known), all being found with their dagger blades present. The Leicester pommel is accompanied only by its flat dagger blade, which has been placed by Piggott with his group of multi-rivet hilt daggers in the flat blade series,[23] relating it to the daggers from Milston and Garton Slack. The almost triangular Lockton Warren blade and the more tongue-shaped Scamridge blade are also flat and can be included in Piggott's flat dagger series. The pommel pieces from Winterbourne Stoke were associated with a massive bronze dagger of the Camerton-Snowshill type (ApSimon 1954, appendix C),[24] showing slight pointillé ornament on the upper part of its pronounced mid-rib. It is likely that the blade and pommel combined to form a magnificent weapon, undoubtedly a symbol of wealth and prestige. Also associated with the pommel were a small bronze knife-dagger (without a pommel), bone tweezers and two fragments of sheet bronze. Apart from their blades and the relatively rich associations of the Winterbourne Stoke piece, the group as a whole is otherwise generally lacking in known associations, being without any record of accompanying pottery.

Group V

The four gold pommel mounts were all found with their dagger blades present, each of which has been included by ApSimon in his group of daggers 'derived from or related to Wessex six-riveted daggers' (ApSimon 1954, appendix B, 56). However, the punched dot decoration forming the ribs of the blade associated with the Blackwaterfoot pommel (Corpus no. 26) also suggests links with the pointillé decoration seen on certain Wessex ogival daggers, and in addition the blade shows an unusual tanged heel formation and two rivets, which is also seen in the blade accompanying the Skateraw mount (Corpus no. 25). The three-riveted blade found with the Collessie mount (Corpus no. 27), although grouped by ApSimon in his appendix B, appears typologically closer to Piggott's flat dagger series. This pommel mount with its accompanying blade were secondary to a primary inhumation containing a beaker classified by Clarke as Northern I Dutch and believed by him to be intrusive and early. The only pottery in direct association with any of the four pommel mounts consists of a single vase type food vessel found with the Topped Mountain piece, and apart from this pot and the blades little else is found in association. The Skateraw and Topped Mountain pieces were found with inhumations, while that from Collessie was from a cremation burial. The Blackwaterfoot pommel does not appear to have had a burial present, which might suggest the possibility that it was associated with an inhumation of which no trace was found during the limited excavation.

Group VI

The associations vary considerably with each pommel, in part reflecting the often exotic and individual nature of the various pieces. Although the funeral rite varies, the Bush Barrow and Shrewton pieces being found with inhumation burials while the Ridgeway gold pommel, the Hammeldon Down and Grange pommels were from cremations, each pommel was found with its dagger blade present. The Bush Barrow pommel (Corpus no. 31) appears to have formed the hilt-end of a blade of almost pure copper (classified by Gerloff as type Ia), accompanying a slightly larger bronze blade of the same type (classified by Gerloff as type Ib).[25] The richness of the pommel and its impressive blade, combined with the valuable assortment of grave goods, suggest a high degree of wealth and social importance of the owner. The accompanying grave goods include a small bronze knife-dagger (which like the larger of the accompanying blades does not have either a pommel or a hilt remaining), a gold belt hook, a polished mace head, bone mounts and a flanged copper axe. The Ridgeway gold pommel (Corpus no. 32) was directly associated with two bronze dagger blades, included by ApSimon in his Bush Barrow type (ApSimon 1954, appendix A, 54), one of which is assumed to have provided the blade for the pommel. Also found in direct association was a small knife-dagger (also without a pommel) and a slightly flanged bronze axe. It is interesting that the gold pommel with its accompanying Bush Barrow type blades is stratigraphically later in the same barrow than the open-ended pommel (Corpus no. 17), yet the blade associated with the latter pommel has been placed by ApSimon in a typologically later group of daggers (appendix B). The Grange pommel (Corpus no. 34) was found with a cremation which was secondary to a burial containing two bowl food vessels and a globular pygmy cup. The pommel was directly associated with a rolled-up, grooved six-riveted dagger blade which has been placed by ApSimon in his group 'derived from or related to Wessex six-riveted daggers' (appendix B, 54). The only association with the Hammeldon Down pommel (Corpus no. 33), apart from its cremation burial, was a fragmentary grooved dagger blade which is included by ApSimon in his group of 'atypical or degenerate daggers related to the Camerton-Snowshill class' (ApSimon 1954, 60). Finally the pommel from Shrewton (Corpus no. 29) was in direct association with a small bronze triangular blade which shows complex workmanship on its ground hollow edges and prominent tang, which contains two rivet holes, one placed vertically above the other. Ashbee[26] and Piggott[27] compare the blade with that from Sittingbourne, describing the blade as a complex development of the tanged or West European flat blade, a type which precedes Piggott's flat dagger groupings. The Shrewton piece is the only West European dagger type in Great Britain with a pommel surviving. It is further unique in that the blade, unlike most of the other West European types known in Great Britain, appears to have been whetted down through use, suggesting a possible functional as well as a probable ornamental use.

Only the Shrewton and Grange pommels in this miscellaneous group are directly associated with pottery, the Grange pommel being found with a cordoned urn, while that from Shrewton accompanies a beaker. The latter has been classified by Clarke as N2 which is early in his series, while Lanting and van der Waals[28] place the pot in category four of their seven stages of beaker development in the Wessex focus area. They support Clarke's early classification, though they note that these beaker types are the latest to be associated with tanged daggers and point out that beakers of this kind appear to be rare in Britain. A secondary burial was accompanied by another beaker classified by Clarke as S4 which is therefore late in his series. The relatively early Shrewton beaker, combined with the small triangular shape of the tanged blade, characteristic of early copper and bronze metallurgy of the Reinecke A phase, provide a powerful argument for a very early pommel and dagger, possibly as a direct continental export,[29] and suggest that the Shrewton piece could well be the earliest of the surviving Early Bronze Age pommels in Great Britain. However it must be borne in mind that there is a possibility of a relatively later date for the Shrewton pommel due to the likely retardation and lingering on of traditions, which appears to be a feature of the associated beaker,[30] and the probable long survival value of the blade.

SECTION FOUR: POSTULATED CHRONOLOGY

At the moment the accepted methods of dating Early Bronze Age assemblages prove to be generally unsatisfactory. In particular pottery typologies and to a lesser extent funerary practices, as a result of the present lack of knowledge, are generally unhelpful guides to either chronology or social grouping. Of the Early Bronze Age pottery types, only beaker pottery has been given a comprehensive typological sequence and a useful general chronology as a result of Clarke's monumental classification, supplemented by the later work of Lanting and van der Waals. In addition with regard to dagger blades the work of Piggott, ApSimon and Gerloff has provided the foundations of a convincing chronological succession of dagger types.

It is not surprising that the problem of absolute dates for the Early Bronze Age in Britain remains a complex and controversial issue. ApSimon among others has postulated absolute dates (ApSimon 1954, 48-51) for his Wessex periods, though it has now become evident that his Wessex chronology appears slightly more complex, with a certain amount of overlapping between his two broad divisions. The absolute dates drawn by ApSimon through correlation of Wessex objects with Mediterranean and Central European parallels might hold good for the object concerned, but as a result of fresh interpretation, particularly with regard to the evidence provided by the halberds, one is justified in extending his beginnings of the Wessex period to $c.$ 1800 B.C. (calibrated to 2100 B.C.). ApSimon's later limit for the Camerton-Snowshill phase can be left unchanged at 1200-1100 B.C. (calibrated to $c.$ 1400 B.C.). Despite slight reservations concerning absolute dates and rigid chronological divisions, it seems reasonable on present evidence to accept these dates as providing the broad chronological horizons for the Early Bronze Age in Britain, within whose limits the corpus of individual pommels can be variously placed. Since the picture presented, in the main, by pottery and dagger types is of a far from simple typological chronology, the construction within this chronological framework of a relative dated sequence of pommels is a difficult matter. Furthermore, the large territory of Early Bronze Age Britain would have permitted in all probability a certain geographic isolation and individualized contact between the regions and with the continent. As a consequence, the dating sequence is made more complex, since both dagger and pommel types show, in certain cases, what are best interpreted as regional differences rather than differences in time.

Not only is there a variety of pommel types from diverse geographic regions, which are sometimes difficult to interrelate, but also in some cases they have been found without associations, or without objects which can be used as chronological pointers. It is also a pity that when a number of the pommels were found the respective excavations or circumstances of removal were not conducted in accordance with modern standards. For example, there appears to be only one group of carbon-14 dates from a find or excavation involving pommels.[31] These dates were obtained from the excavation of Bedd Branwen. A sample was taken from charcoal found with cremated bones probably belonging to pot B, which contained a Group II pommel (Corpus no. 13). This gave a calibrated date of c. 1600 B.C., which dates the probable interment of the pommel into the barrow.

Since it is accepted that the basic idea of making a metal blade and separate hilt-piece did come from outside Britain, with it no doubt came the idea of the pommel. As the pommel types found on the continent have not been studied (to the writer's knowledge no corpus of European pommels at present exists), it is hypothetically assumed that the earliest European pommels are parental to the British pieces. Therefore, following the accepted pottery and dagger morphologies, which begin the British series with the introduction of European prototypes in the form of early intrusive beakers and West European dagger types, there are strong grounds for suggesting that the Shrewton pommel with its accompanying, slightly developed West European blade and early beaker type is the earliest pommel found in Britain, and might itself be a continental import. With the unlikely exception of the pommel and hilt-piece from the copper blade found in Bush Barrow, there appears to be no other evidence of likely importation from the continent, which suggests the remaining body of pommels were of insular British manufacture, and are therefore later in date.

If it is thus accepted as the earliest pommel in Britain with a probable dating close to the opening of the Early Bronze Age, the Shrewton pommel can be assumed to provide a starting date of around 2000 B.C. for the series. It is possible to see certain of the pommel groupings as having a measure of chronological significance without necessarily believing in rigid typological chronologies. The large trough types of group I consistently appear to be relatively early, possibly emerging not long after the Shrewton pommel since all were associated with flat daggers and accompanying inhumations, and include a fairly late beaker found with the Ashgrove pommel (Corpus no. 1). Similarly, two pommels from Group III, those from Eynsham (Corpus no. 18) and Garrowby Wold (Corpus no. 19), both from inhumations and associated with flat daggers, can also be considered early in relation to the Shrewton pommel, particularly as the Eynsham piece is accompanied by a fairly late beaker type. The close relationship of the open-ended Ridgeway pommel (Corpus no. 17) to the Eynsham piece, coupled with the Ridgeway pommel's early associations, might also, despite a possible later blade type, suggest a similarly early date. The closest typological variant to the Shrewton pommel appears to be the pommel from Leicester (Corpus no. 24) which, with its flat blade and inhumation burial might suggest that it is a slightly earlier date in relation to the Shrewton piece than the pommels of Group I. Of the other composite pommels, the closely related Lockton Warren (Corpus no. 21) and Scamridge (Corpus no. 22) examples, both with flat blades, can also be placed with the above mentioned pommels in the early part of the chronological spectrum.

The pommels of Groups II and IIa, with the exception of the two Wessex pieces which show a far richer variety of associated objects, are consistently from cremation burials in association with an urn of some kind, features which are possibly not entirely indicative of a later date within the overall chronological structure. These pommels show a marked regional grouping into the highland areas of North Wales and the Pennines, and could be regarded rather as a local tradition, which might be reasonably contemporary with the earlier groups of pommels. However it seems more likely, particularly as the carbon-14 date from Bedd Branwen is relatively late, that these pommels can be placed in the later part of the Early Bronze Age.

The amber pommel from the Manton Barrow (Corpus no. 7) appears to be contemporary with the earlier groups of pommels, since it was found in an inhumation burial with an early flat knife blade in association with a pendant which, it has been suggested, is a copy of the early metal-shafted halberds of Central Europe. However, ApSimon[32] argues that the Manton burial is late on the basis of the gold bound amber discs, which he regards as a British product and parallels with a similar disc found in a late grave at Knossos. He supports this later dating by describing the incense cup as 'degenerate' and therefore late, and suggests that the pommel may have had an heirloom value with the probable long survival of the blade. However it is doubtful whether he is justified in using a Cretan date to provide a precise English chronology, on the grounds of distance. The Winterbourne Stoke pommel (Corpus no. 16) is associated with a knife-dagger showing slight mid-rib markings, which implies it is a later blade type than the simple flat daggers. This suggests, therefore, that the pommel is probably later than those associated with the flat dagger blades, and could well be given a similar dating to the other pommels of Group II.

The group of gold pommel mounts appears to represent a broad regional grouping, and it is tempting to suggest that the mounts also comprise a fairly compact chronological group, on the grounds of their close stylistic similarity and the fact that they are all associated with blades classified by ApSimon as 'Bush Barrow derived'. It is likely that these pommel mounts are later than the geographically close Group I pommel from Ashgrove, with its associated flat dagger blade and beaker. However it is possible that the difference in time between these pommel mounts and the earlier pommels associated with flat blades is not great, as the blade associated with the Skateraw mount appears closely related to the flat dagger types. It would also follow on the basis of blade typology, that the mounts would be in general slightly later than the pommels associated with the true Bush Barrow blade types in Wessex, especially since it is likely that Wessex was probably the originating source for such blades in Britain. Consequently the group might be safely placed in the chronological spectrum at points later than the early pommels associated with flat blades, and slightly later than the pommels found with Bush Barrow blades.

It also appears reasonable to suggest a comparable position in time for the other Irish pommel, that from Grange (Corpus no. 34), which is similarly associated with a 'Bush Barrow derived' blade. However such a dating might possibly be questioned on the grounds of the pommel's similar basic design to that of the Hammeldon Down pommel, which appears to be late in the series.

The Bush Barrow pommel and the Ridgeway gold pommel are possibly reasonably contemporary with each other, since both are associated with Bush Barrow type blades, and show certain stylistic links. In particular, the Ridgeway pommel's incised decoration can be compared with the decoration of the belt hook cover found in Bush Barrow, and the chevron motif around the lip of the Ridgeway pommel can be paralleled by the decorative effect of the pin arrangement on the Bush Barrow pommel. On the evidence of the Amesbury pommel amongst other examples, which was associated with a flat blade of Piggott's series and was primary in the barrow to a later burial associated with a Bush Barrow type blade, it seems in general that the Bush Barrow type blades appear to be later than the flat varieties. Despite the probable occurrence of a certain degree of chronological overlapping, it seems a safe assumption that the Bush Barrow and Ridgeway gold pommels can be placed slightly later on the chronological scale than the early pommels of Groups I, III and IV, which were found with flat blades accompanying inhumations; while on the other hand these two pommels are probably earlier than the gold mounts of Group V.

The Stanton Moor pommel (Corpus no. 20) with its rather sophisticated design and typologically late blade suggest the pommel is of late date. Similarly the Winterbourne Stoke pommel (Corpus no. 23) appears to be late, since it is the only pommel found accompanying a true Camerton-Snowshill type blade. The Hammeldon Down pommel (Corpus no. 33) appears also to be late, since the pommel shows a sophisticated design and its blade, though fragmentary has been included by ApSimon in his 'atypical or degenerate' Camerton-Snowshill group (ApSimon 1954, 60). These three pommels appear to be the latest of the corpus of known pommels in Britain, representing probably the last phases of pommel development in the Early Bronze Age.

They can probably be dated close to 1600 B.C., and provide the upper chronological limit to the pommel series, extending back to the Shrewton piece situated at a chronological point close to the beginnings of British bronze working.

Finally, note should be made of two apparent chronological anomalies: firstly the blade associated with the Bush Barrow pommel and hilt-piece is of almost pure copper and therefore should ideally be very early in any British dagger sequence, whereas the blade type and its associations suggest that it is contemporary with other Wessex Bush Barrow types, and is probably later in the sequence than the bronze flat daggers. A second possible anomaly concerns the Ridgeway gold pommel, which with its true Bush Barrow type blade is stratigraphically later than the open-ended pommel associated with a 'Bush Barrow derived' blade. This apparent reversal of typological sequence, combined with the typologically late flanged axe associated with the gold pommel, might suggest that the pommel was an heirloom which had a long survival value before being consigned to the grave.[33]

The apparent difficulties in providing a rigid chronological sequence for the various pommels reflect present inadequacies in understanding the full chronological significance of the pottery and dagger typologies, and emphasise the confused situation regarding absolute dates for the Early Bronze Age. This chronological uncertainty is not eased by the fact that many of the pommels and their daggers appear to have had a long survival value, and it is very probable that certain of the types would have been in use at the same time.

SECTION FIVE: STYLISTIC AFFINITIES WITHIN THE CORPUS

The pommel types grouped empirically on the basis of style, method of attachment and material used are, it is admitted, not of particularly great value in terms of chronology. However, it is possible to see certain stylistic links between the pommels which might represent some contact, be it trade or migration of peoples, within the different regions of Britain.

The trough pommels of Groups I and II represent the most common and most widely distributed pommel type in Early Bronze Age Britain, perhaps as a consequence of the pommel type being probably the easiest and least sophisticated way of adding an end-cap to the hilt. The unique Shrewton pommel, though earlier than these trough types, appears stylistically more complex and represents a higher degree of competence in its workmanship. As already noted the early dating for the Leicester pommel is postulated almost solely on its limited stylistic affinity with the Shrewton piece. The Leicester pommel also represents a simple method of pommel attachment, substituting the construction of a pommel hilt-end receptacle for a simple metal blade attached between the two halves of the pommel mount which is then riveted to the hilt. This bronze tang probably extended to the heel of the blade, though Evans[34] is of the opinion it did not, creating a multi-rivet hilt effect similar to that of the Milston and Garton Slack pieces, thereby adding weight to the already postulated early date for the latter daggers' pommels and therefore the others of Group I.

Stylistically the smaller Group II pommels with their characteristic overhanging lip, have in this respect closer relations with the Shrewton pommel than do the group I type. The three pommels from Group IIa (Corpus nos. 14, 15 and 16) showing pommel top perforations are arguably a more typologically complex pommel than their simple trough type relatives, since attachment with added top pins (if top pins were used) would be slightly more difficult. It has been suggested that the circular holes in the pommel top might have fitted over projections from the hilt-end tang,[35] though it is

45

unlikely that this would have occurred with the very small pommels, such as that from Bedd Branwen (Corpus no. 14).

The open-ended pommels of Group III also represent a stylistic development on the trough type, and possibly evolved as a result of an error in the manufacture of the trough pommel, by continuing the hilt-end receptacle too far, and opening the pommel top. The upper opening in the pommels from Barrow 7, the Ridgeway (Corpus no. 17) and Eynsham (Corpus no. 18) would have been filled by the tooled top of the hilt-end tang, fitting flush with the pommel top. This would have afforded an attractive contrast of the white bone of the pommel surrounding the probably darker coloured inlay of the hilt top.[36] In the case of the Garrowby Wold pommel (Corpus no. 19) and more particularly that from Stanton Moor (Corpus no. 20), it is possible that an extension from the hilt-end tang projected some way out of the pommel, possibly in the shape of a dome or decorative knob.

Of the composite pieces of Group IV the pommels from Scamridge (Corpus no. 22) and Lockton Warren (Corpus no. 21) have affinities in shape and size with the trough type of Group I, representing, in effect, an alternative method of constructing a 'trough' pommel. It has been suggested that the pommels were originally decorated by projecting tongues of wood from the top of the hilt piece tenon.[37] However, cut out from the central pommel component is a mortised receptacle designed to accommodate a hilt-end tang, and therefore, if additional tongues of wood were present, construction of the hilt-end must have been a difficult process. This cannot be properly ascertained in the case of the Lockton Warren pommel because of the latter's bad condition. However, the Scamridge piece appears to be almost perfectly preserved, with its two upper metal pins still surviving and appearing exactly to span the width of the pommel. Therefore, assuming the pommel and pins not to have been tampered with, the piece does not appear to have room to accommodate additional tongues of wood. The bone quadrants of the massive pommel mount from Winterbourne Stoke G.4 (Corpus no. 23) probably exhibit a similar principle to that found in the Ridgeway and Eynsham pommels, of contrasting inlays, employed in a more impressive and unique manner. The corresponding alternate quadrants do not survive, suggesting they were made of wood, and possibly constituted part of the handle, the wood being darker than the bone mounts creating an attractive contrast in the shape of a cruciform pattern, which suggests affinities with the cruciform pin pattern on the similarly late Hammeldon Down amber pommel (Corpus no. 33).

The Bush Barrow pommel and hilt-piece appear to be the only direct British parallel to the European inlaid gold pin hilts. The tiny decorative pins, which appear to be in no way functional, creating an intricate and complex design, represent a valuable work of the highest craftsmanship, unique among British pommels, which, combined with its impressive blade, made it undoubtedly a symbol of wealth and prestige. The Ridgeway gold pommel has certain affinities with the Bush Barrow pommel and its associations, however it is worth noting that the Ridgeway pommel's pins are in no way decorative, but are purely functional. They are also much larger than the more numerous Bush Barrow pins and appear nearer in size to the pins found on the La Garenne piece.[38]

Stylistically affiliated in certain respects to the Ridgeway gold pommel are the four strikingly similar gold pommel mounts from Scotland and Ireland (Corpus nos. 25-28), all being crafted, like the Ridgeway piece, from sheet gold and bearing similar decoration to the incised, concentric grooves of the collar and top piece of the Ridgeway pommel, the decoration probably being obtained by a similar technique. However, there are differences, as firstly the pommel mounts differ in principle from the completely enclosing Ridgeway pommel, consisting simply of a decorative gold collar; and secondly the mounts do not employ the chevron motif in their decoration. Miss Henshall in her description of the mounts makes no mention of pins, pin-holes, nor pitch or other adhesive substance being found inside the collars.[39] In fact the exact position of the collars, the type of pommel and hilt to which they were fastened and the exact method of attachment is not known. Attachment was probably by means of the flanged edges, the mounts being hammered into place, probably around the pommel neck, in the manner of a spring-clip. The original oblong shape of the Collessie mount suggests that it might have had a pommel similar to those of Group I, in particular similar to that from Ashgrove, which seems very likely as both Collessie and Ashgrove are situated geographically very close together in the county of Fife.

The Hammeldon Down amber pommel (Corpus no. 33) with its inlaid gold pin decoration, represents an adaptation of the Bush Barrow pommel's gold pin decorative technique applied more simply to a harder, more exotic medium. The pins like those of the Ridgeway pommel, are larger and more substantial than those from the Bush Barrow piece, but unlike the Ridgeway pins are purely decorative in function, with the exception of the seven repair pins. The amber pommel can also be compared with the pommel from Grange (Corpus no. 34) in method of attachment, each pommel exhibiting a complex arrangement designed in part to leave no attachment pins visible on the outer surface of the pommel. It is also worth noting that the Ridgeway gold pommel, that from Hammeldon Down, and the piece from Grange are all reasonably similar in general shape and size.

GENERAL CONCLUSIONS

Perhaps the most outstanding conclusion one can draw from the corpus concerns the pommels of Group II, with the exception of the two Wessex pieces. None of these pommels, from the highland regions of North Wales and the Pennines, has been found with a blade in association, and in fact it can be reasonably doubted that these eight pommels were consigned to the grave with metal blades since not one blade survives, nor is evidenced as having existed in the grave. This makes them distinctive on two accounts: firstly in every other case where a pommel has been found, it has been in association with a metal blade. Secondly they represent a direct reversal of the general Early Bronze Age tendency to consign a blade to the grave without its pommel. This lack of evidence for a blade cannot be Bedd Branwen[40] was excavated as recently as 1967 and the results strongly suggest that the blades were not interred as funerary goods. The small size and often irregular nature of the hilt-end receptacle suggests that the pommels would have been suitable for only the smallest knife-dagger, similar in size perhaps to a small modern table knife. It is difficult to imagine the function of these knives, unless they belonged to women or were children's toys, which judging from the burials does not seem to be the case. More probably, since these pommels show a distinct regional distribution, they represent a regional tradition, perhaps originated through economic necessity, where the blade was not interred with the body. Possibly the blade was too valuable to sacrifice and these pommels might represent the surviving part of a special funerary model, the hilt and blade possibly being made of a perishable substance such as wood and not therefore surviving. The existence of a dagger blade made completely of bone found at Crug y Afon[41] might support this argument. Furthermore although the pommels exhibit pinhole perforations none has present its holding pins, suggesting either that they too were made of wood and have perished, or that pins were not used for attachment.

The pommels of Groups V and VI might in certain cases be interpreted as representing possible characteristics of other pommel types such as style or size, translated perhaps into a more exotic or valuable material, or given a more complex method of attachment: compare the shape and size of the Gristhorpe pommel (Corpus no. 6) with the Ridgeway gold pommel (Corpus no. 28), or the continuation of the hilt line in the pommel edge in the Bush Barrow reconstruction (Corpus no. 27) with the similar line in the Milston hilt and pommel (Corpus no. 4). Conversely, Group II includes the Manton amber pommel (Corpus no. 7), amber being probably a rare and valuable trade object, and found only in one other pommel from the south of England.

It is preferable to see the pommels more in a regional, if not a local context, as overall comparisons and conclusions may lead to weighted values. It is obvious that though the pommel corpus by its limited number and nature represents only a tiny aspect of the Early Bronze Age culture, it reflects to some extent the equality of the cultures found in other regions with that of the local culture of Wessex. The Wessex pommels in certain instances are more spectacular, but the overall distribution of pommels reflects, not the dominance of the Wessex culture, but the parallel cultural development of the diverse regions of Britain.

Very few pommels have come to light as compared with the relatively large number of daggers known to exist, regarding which, in the light of present knowledge, no decisive reasons can be given. However, it is worth noting that examples from a variety of regions such as Corston Beacon in Pembrokeshire, the Bush Barrow type dagger from Amesbury 85, Wiltshire and certain Scottish daggers such as that from Wasbister (Orkney) and Auchterhouse (Angus) all appear to have hilts surviving, but are without pommels. In these cases particularly, and possibly in others where there are no hilt remains, such is the rarity of pommels that there is jusitification in the belief that for some reason the pommels were deliberately detached before consigning the blade and possibly the hilt to the grave.

Finally, it is also possible that a certain number of Early Bronze Age dagger blades were affixed to perishable hilts made in one piece, without a separate pommel, which would in part account for so few pommels surviving in relation to the relatively large number of extant dagger blades. This possibility suggests, therefore, that pommels could well be the exception rather than the rule in the Early Bronze Age.

APPENDIX

Table showing the principal associations found with British Early Bronze Age Dagger Pommels.

Corpus No.	Pommel Location	Pommel Group	Size[1]	Blade Type[2]	Inhumation	Cremation	Beaker	Food Vessel	Urn	Additional Associations and Notes
1	Ashgrove, Methilhill, Fife	I	44 mm x 16 mm	Flat	X		X (s4)			Blade interred with its sheath.
2	Barrow 85, Boscombe Down, Amesbury, Wilts.	I	40 mm ?	Flat	X					Secondary cremation in the barrow containing knife-dagger & Bush Barrow type dagger.
3	Helperthorpe, Yorks.	I	48 mm x 14 mm	Flat	X					
4	Milston, Grave 51, Wilts.	I	44 mm x 14 mm	Flat	X					Multi-rivet hilt containing additional pointille decoration.
5	Garton Slack, Barrow 107, Yorks.	I	49 mm x 14 mm	Flat	X (Secondary)			X (?)		Copper or bronze armlet.
6	Gristhorpe, near Scarborough, Yorks.	I	52 mm x 20 mm	Flat	X					Interred in a large oak trunk coffin.
7	'Manton Barrow', Preshute, Grave 1a, Wilts.	II	22 mm x 10 mm	Flat	X (Female)				X (Collared)	Grape cup, gold-bound amber discs, pointille incense cup, awl, beads, halberd pendant.
8	Galley Low, Brassington Moor, Derbyshire.	II	32.5 mm x 10 mm	No Blade	X				X (Collared)	Flint arrowhead.
9	Narrowdale Hill, Alstonfield, Staffs.	II	19.5 mm x 12 mm	No Blade		X			X	Cordoned urn, flint arrowhead.
10	Merddyn Gwyn, Pentraeth, Anglesey	II	33 mm x 10 mm	No Blade		X (Secondary) (Female)			X (Enlarged)	
11	Bwlch y Rhiw, Caerns.	II	27 mm x 9 mm	No Blade		X			X (Collared)	Bronze awl.
12	Wilmslow, Cheshire.	II	35 mm x 10 mm	No Blade		X			X	
13	Bedd Branwen Llanbabo, Anglesey.	II	35 mm x 10 mm	No Blade		X (Secondary)			X (Collared)	Whetstone.
14	Bedd Branwen, Llanbabo, Anglesey.	IIa	30 mm x 5 mm	No Blade		X			X (Collared)	Amber, jet and bone beads.
15	Marian Bach, Cwm, Flints.	IIa	28.5 mm x 5 mm	No Blade		X (Secondary)			X (Collared)	
16	Winterbourne Stoke, Grave 66, Wilts.	IIa	34 mm x 10 mm	Knife-Dagger related to Camerton-Snowshill types (?)		X			X (Collared)	Beads.
17	Barrow 7, The Ridgeway, Dorset.	III	32.5 mm x 13.5 mm	'Bush Barrow derived' (?)	X (Secondary)					Knife-dagger, stone mace head, flint axe. (see Pommel No. 32)
18	Foxley Farm, Eynsham, Oxford.	III	44 mm x 12 mm	Flat	X		X (F.P.)			Tubular beads.
19	Garrowby Wold, Barrow 32, Yorks.	III	44 mm x 12 mm	Flat	X	X				Beaker found in the same barrow.
20	Stanton Moor, Birchover, Derbyshire.	III	34 mm x 10 mm	Leaf Shaped Blade, with slightly decorated mid-rib		X			X	Bronze pin, bone pin, flint scrapers.
21	Lockton Warren, Yorks.	IV	50 mm x 21 mm	Flat	(?)					
22	Scamridge, near Pickering, Yorks.	IV	52 mm x 18 mm	Flat	X					Flint scrapers.
23	Winterbourne Stoke, Grave 4, Wilts.	IV	68 mm (?) x 13 mm	Camerton-Snowshill		X				Knife-dagger, bone tweezers, pin, all in bronze bound elm chest.
24	Leicester.	IV	45 mm x 14 mm	Flat	X					
25	Skateraw, East Lothian.	V	38 mm x 4 mm	'Bush Barrow derived'	X					Blade in sheath.
26	Blackwaterfoot, Arran.	V	41 mm x 5 mm	Ribbed flat Blade - 'Bush Barrow derived' (?)	(?)					
27	Gask Hill, Collessie, Fife.	V	30 mm x 7 mm	'Bush Barrow derived'		X (Secondary)				Blade in sheath. Secondary to an inhumation burial with N.I.D. beaker.
28	Topped Mountain, Co. Fermanagh.	V	39 mm x 6 mm	'Bush Barrow derived'	X			X (Vase)		Cremation burial (?) in same cist.
29	Nett Down, Barrow 5K, Shrewton, Wilts.	VI	40 mm x 25 mm	Tanged or West European type	X		X (n.2)			S4 Beaker secondary.
31	'Bush Barrow', Grave 5, Normanton, Wilts.	VI	60 mm (?) x 20 mm	Copper Bush Barrow type Blade						Bronze Bush Barrow type blade, mace head, sheet gold lozenge plates, gold belt hook, copper axe, bronze hook, bone mounts, k-dagger.
32	Barrow 7, The Ridgeway, Dorset.	VI	55 mm x 19 mm	Bush Barrow type		X				Additional Bush Barrow type dagger, knife-dagger, flanged bronze axe. (see Pommel No. 17)
33	Hammeldon Down, Devon.	VI	60 mm x 14 mm	Atypical or degenerate Dagger related to Camerton-Snowshill type		X				
34	Grange, Co. Roscommon.	VI	45 mm x 15 mm	'Bush Barrow derived'		X (Secondary)			X	Primary burial contained a pygmy cup and two food vessels.

in relation to the relatively large number of extant dagger blades. This possibility suggests, therefore, that pommels could well be the exception rather than the rule in the Early Bronze Age.

APPENDIX

Table showing the principal associations found with British Early Bronze Age Dagger Pommels.

Corpus No.	Pommel Location	Pommel Group	Size[1]	Blade Type[2]	Inhumation	Cremation	Beaker	Food Vessel	Urn	Additional Associations and Notes
1	Ashgrove, Methilhill, Fife	I	44 mm x 16 mm	Flat	X		X (s4)			Blade interred with its sheath.
2	Barrow 85, Boscombe Down, Amesbury, Wilts.	I	40 mm ?	Flat	X					Secondary cremation in the barrow containing knife-dagger & Bush Barrow type dagger.
3	Helperthorpe, Yorks.	I	48 mm x 14 mm	Flat	X					
4	Milston, Grave 51, Wilts.	I	44 mm x 14 mm	Flat	X					Multi-rivet hilt containing additional pointillé decoration.
5	Garton Slack, Barrow 107, Yorks.	I	49 mm x 14 mm	Flat	X (Secondary)			X (?)		Copper or bronze armlet.
6	Gristhorpe, near Scarborough, Yorks.	I	52 mm x 20 mm	Flat	X					Interred in a large oak trunk coffin.
7	'Manton Barrow', Preshute, Grave 1a, Wilts.	II	22 mm x 10 mm	Flat	X (Female)				X (Collared)	Grape cup, gold-bound amber discs, pointillé incense cup, awl, beads, halberd pendant.
8	Galley Low, Brassington Moor, Derbyshire.	II	32.5 mm x 10 mm	No Blade	X				X (Collared)	Flint arrowhead.
9	Narrowdale Hill, Alstonfield, Staffs.	II	19.5 mm x 12 mm	No Blade		X			X	Cordoned urn, flint arrowhead.
10	Merddyn Gwyn, Pentraeth, Anglesey	II	33 mm x 10 mm	No Blade		X (Secondary) (Female)		X (Enlarged)		
11	Bwlch y Rhiw, Caerns.	II	27 mm x 9 mm	No Blade		X			X (Collared)	Bronze awl.
12	Wilmslow, Cheshire.	II	35 mm x 10 mm	No Blade		X			X	
13	Bedd Branwen, Llanbabo, Anglesey.	II	35 mm x 10 mm	No Blade		X (Secondary)			X (Collared)	Whetstone.
14	Bedd Branwen, Llanbabo, Anglesey.	IIa	30 mm x 5 mm	No Blade		X			X (Collared)	Amber, jet and bone beads.
15	Marian Bach, Cwm, Flints.	IIa	28.5 mm x 5 mm	No Blade		X (Secondary)			X (Collared)	
16	Winterbourne Stoke, Grave 66, Wilts.	IIa	34 mm x 10 mm	Knife-Dagger related to Camerton-Snowshill types (?)		X			X (Collared)	Beads.
17	Barrow 7, The Ridgeway, Dorset.	III	32.5 mm x 13.5 mm	'Bush Barrow derived' (?)	X (Secondary)					Knife-dagger, stone mace head, flint axe. (see Pommel No. 32)
18	Foxley Farm, Eynsham, Oxford.	III	44 mm x 12 mm	Flat	X			X (F.P.)		Tubular beads.
19	Garrowby Wold, Barrow 32, Yorks.	III	44 mm x 12 mm	Flat	X	X				Beaker found in the same barrow.
20	Stanton Moor, Birchover, Derbyshire.	III	34 mm x 10 mm	Leaf Shaped Blade, with slightly decorated mid-rib		X			X	Bronze pin, bone pin, flint scrapers.
21	Lockton Warren, Yorks.	IV	50 mm x 21 mm	Flat	(?)					
22	Scamridge, near Pickering, Yorks.	IV	52 mm x 18 mm	Flat	X					Flint scrapers.
23	Winterbourne Stoke, Grave 4, Wilts.	IV	68 mm (?) x 13 mm	Camerton-Snowshill		X				Knife-dagger, bone tweezers, pin, all in bronze bound elm chest.
24	Leicester.	IV	45 mm x 14 mm	Flat	X					
25	Skateraw, East Lothian.	V	38 mm x 4 mm	'Bush Barrow derived'	X					Blade in sheath.
26	Blackwaterfoot, Arran.	V	41 mm x 5 mm	Ribbed flat Blade - 'Bush Barrow derived' (?)	(?)					
27	Gask Hill, Collessie, Fife.	V	30 mm x 7 mm	'Bush Barrow derived'		X (Secondary)				Blade in sheath. Secondary to an inhumation burial with N.I.D. beaker.
28	Topped Mountain, Co. Fermanagh.	V	39 mm x 6 mm	'Bush Barrow derived'	X			X (Vase)		Cremation burial (?) in same cist.
29	Nett Down, Barrow 5K, Shrewton, Wilts.	VI	40 mm x 25 mm	Tanged or West European type	X		X (n.2)			S4 Beaker secondary.
31	'Bush Barrow', Grave 5, Normanton, Wilts.	VI	60 mm (?) x 20 mm	Copper Bush Barrow type Blade						Bronze Bush Barrow type blade, mace head, sheet gold lozenge plates, gold belt hook, copper axe, bronze hook, bone mounts, k-dagger.
32	Barrow 7, The Ridgeway, Dorset.	VI	55 mm x 19 mm	Bush Barrow type		X				Additional Bush Barrow type dagger, knife-dagger, flanged bronze axe. (see Pommel No. 17)
33	Hammeldon Down, Devon.	VI	60 mm x 14 mm	Atypical or degenerate Dagger related to Camerton-Snowshill type		X				
34	Grange, Co. Roscommon.	VI	45 mm x 15 mm	'Bush Barrow derived'		X (Secondary)			X	Primary burial contained a pygmy cup and two food vessels.

Notes: 1. The upper figure refers to the length across the pommel top, and the lower to the vertical depth of the pommel measured from the top to the base of the hilt-end socket.

2. Dagger Blade Types:
   a. Flat blade types: the dagger blades included by Piggott in his typological groupings of flat blades, without mid-rib or blade markings. Piggott 1963, 82-88.
   b. Bush Barrow Type: as classified in ApSimon 1954, Appendix A, 54.
   c. 'Bush Barrow Derived': classified as 'Derived from or related to Wessex six-riveted daggers' in ApSimon 1954, Appendix B, 56.
   d. Camerton-Snowshill: classified as 'ogival type' in ApSimon 1954, Appendix C, 59.

BIBLIOGRAPHY

Annable and Simpson 1964	F. K. Annable and D. D. A. Simpson, Guide Catalogue of the neolithic and Bronze Age Collections in Devizes Museum (1964).
ApSimon 1954	A. M. ApSimon, "Dagger Graves in the 'Wessex' Bronze Age", Tenth Annual Report, Institute of Archaeology, London (1954), 37-61.
Ashbee 1957	P. Ashbee, "The Great Barrow at Bishop's Waltham", Proceedings of the Prehistoric Society, XXXIII (1957), 164-5.
Ashbee 1960	P. Ashbee, The Bronze Age Round Barrow in Britain (1960).
Bateman 1848	T. W. Bateman, Vestiges of the Antiquities of Derbyshire (1848).
Bateman 1861	T. W. Bateman, Ten Years Diggings in Celtic and Saxon Grave Hills in the counties of Derby, Stafford and York from 1848-58, (1861).
British Museum 1920	A Guide to the Antiquities of the Bronze Age in the Department of British and Medieval Antiquities. British Museum (1920).
Burgess 1962-4	C. B. Burgess, "Two grooved ogival daggers of the Early Bronze Age from South Wales", Bulletin of the Board of Celtic Studies, XX(1962-4), 78-82.
Case 1966	H. J. Case, "Were Beaker-People the First Metallurgists in Ireland?", Paleohistoria, XII, 141-177 (1966).
Childe 1946	V. G. Childe, Scotland before the Scots (1946), 119, 121.
Clarke 1970	D. L. Clarke, Beaker Pottery of Great Britain and Ireland (1970).
Coles and Taylor 1971	J. Coles and J. J. Taylor, "The Wessex Culture: a minimal view", Antiquity, XIV (1971), 6-14.
Drew and Piggott 1936	C. D. Drew and S. Piggott, "Two Bronze Age Barrows excavated by Mr Edward Cunnington. Proceedings of the Dorset Natural History and Archaeological Society, LVII (1936), 20-1, 24-5.
Evans 1881	Sir J. Evans, The ancient bronze implements, weapons and ornaments of Great Britain and Ireland (1881).

Gerloff 1972	S. Gerloff, Classification of "Wessex Culture" Daggers in *Bronze Age Metalwork in Salisbury Museum*, ed. Moore and Rowlands (1972), 10-11.
Greenwell and Rolleston 1877	*British Barrows* (1877).
Grinsell 1959	L. V. Grinsell, *Dorset Barrows* (1959)
Harbison 1968	P. Harbison, "Catalogue of Irish Early Bronze Age Associated Finds containing copper or bronze", *Proceedings of the Royal Irish Academy*, 67 (1968), 51.
Harbison 1969	P. Harbison, "Daggers and Halberds of the Early Bronze Age in Ireland", *Prähistorische Bronzefunde*, VI (1969).
Henshall 1963-4	A. S. Henshall, "A dagger grave and other cist burials at Ashgrove, Methilhill, Fife", *Proceedings of the Society of Antiquaries of Scotland*, 1963-4.
Henshall 1968	A. S. Henshall, "Scottish Dagger Graves", in *Studies in Ancient Europe, Essays presented to Stuart Piggott*, ed. J. M. Coles and D. D. A. Simpson (1968).
Hoare 1810	R. C. Hoare, *Ancient Wiltshire*, vol. I (1810).
Howarth 1899	ed. E. Howarth, *Catalogue of the Bateman Collection of Antiquities in the Sheffield Public Museum* (1899).
Hughes 1908	H. Hughes, "Merddyn Gwyn, Anglesey", *Archaeologia Cambrensis*, (1908), 211-20.
Inventaria 1956	*Inventaria Archaeologica*, 1956, no. GB 14: Grave Groups and Hoards of the British Bronze Age (2), ed. M. A. Smith.
Kendrick 1937	T. D. Kendrick, "The Hammeldon Down Pommel", *Antiquaries Journal*, XVII (1937), 313-4.
Lanting and van der Waals 1972	J. N. Lanting and J. D. van der Waals, "British Beakers as seen from the continent", *Helinium* 12 (1972), 20-46.
Lynch 1970	F. M. Lynch, *Prehistoric Anglesey* (1970).
Lynch 1971	F. M. Lynch, "Report on the Re-excavation of two Bronze Age Cairns in Anglesey: Bedd Branwen and Treiorwerth", *Archaeologia Cambrensis*, 120 (1971), 11-83.
Moore and Rowlands 1972	C. N. Moore and M. Rowlands, *Bronze Age Metal Work in Salisbury Museum* (1972).

Mortimer 1905	J. R. Mortimer, Forty Years Researches in British and Saxon Burial Mounds of East Yorkshire (1905).
Piggott 1938	S. Piggott, "The Early Bronze Age in Wessex", Proceedings of the Prehistoric Society, IV, part I (1938), 52-106.
Piggott 1963	S. Piggott, "Abercromby and After. The Beaker Cultures of Britain Re-examined" in Culture and Environment, ed. Foster and Alcock (1963).
R. C. A. M. (Caerns) 1964	Royal Commission for Ancient Monuments, Caernarvonshire, III (1964)
Stone 1958	J. F. S. Stone, Wessex before the Celts (1958)
Taylor 1970	J. J. Taylor, "The recent discovery of gold pins in the Ridgeway gold pommel", Antiquaries Journal, L, part II (1970), 216-221.
Thomas 1965-66	N. Thomas, "Notes on some Early Bronze Age objects in Devizes Museum", Wiltshire Archaeological Magazine, 61 (1965-66), 1-8.
Thurnham 1870	J. Thurnham, "On Ancient British Barrows", Archaeologia XLIII (1870), 280-5.
Thurnham and Davis 1856	J. Thurnham and J. Davis, Crania Britannica (1856).
Williamson 1872	W. C. Williamson, Tumulus opened at Gristhorpe, Scarborough (1872).

REFERENCES

1. This is the number of pommels known in Britain up to December 1973.
2. Evans 1881, 232.
3. Hoare 1810, 124; and noted by Evans 1881, 231.
4. This piece is now no longer extant. It is described by Evans 1881, 231, and fig. 290.
5. Evans 1881, 232, fig. 285.
6. This is suggested by Evans 1881, 230.
7. The blade has been classified by ApSimon 1954, appendix B, 56, as belonging to a group 'derived from or related to Bush Barrow types'.
8. Included by Piggott 1963 in group II of his flat blade series.
9. ApSimon 1954, appendix C, 57.
10. This suggestion has been persuasively put forward by N. Thomas 1965-66, 6.
11. Evans 1881, 231, appears to be of the opinion that the bronze pommel tang did not extend to the butt of the blade, nor served as a centre plate for the hilt.
12. Both of the six-rivet blades associated with the Ridgeway gold pommel have been classified as Bush Barrow type by ApSimon 1954, appendix A, 54, and by Gerloff (in Moore and Rowlands 1972, 10) who places the blades with her type Ia.
13. The two six-rivet blades have been classified by ApSimon 1954, appendix A, 54, and exemplify his Bush Barrow type. Gerloff (in Moore and Rowlands 1972, 10) classifies the copper blade as type Ia of her Armorico-British daggers, and the larger bronze blade as type Ib.
14. The blade has been classified by ApSimon 1954, appendix B, 56, as 'Bush Barrow derived'.
15. The blade accompanying the Hammeldon Down pommel has been included by ApSimon 1954, 60, in his group of 'Atypical or degenerate daggers related to Camerton-Snowshill type daggers'.
16. The Grange dagger is described by Harbison 1968, 51, as being of his Topped Mt. type. ApSimon 1954, appendix B, 56, places the blade with his group 'derived from or related to Wessex six-rivet daggers'.
17. Piggott 1963, 82-85, provides a classification for flat daggers.
18. Moore and Rowlands 1972, 38.
19. This is suggested by Ashbee 1960, 102.
20. Ibid., appendix B, 56.
21. Ibid., appendix A, 54.

22. Lanting and van der Waals, 1972, 37, fig. I.

23. Ibid., 84.

24. Ibid., 54.

25. Gerloff's classification is now published in Moore and Rowlands 1972, 10.

26. Ashbee 1960, 98.

27. Piggott 1963, 82.

28. Lanting and van der Waals 1972, 36, 37 and fig. I.

29. Case 1966, 157 has suggested that the Shrewton blade might be an import from Central Europe, basing his argument in part on the blade's high arsenic content (see also Moore and Rowlands 1972, appendix B, 38).

30. This is suggested by Lanting and van der Waals 1972, 43.

31. Lynch 1971, appendix VIII, 82. The excavator published four carbon-14 samples from Bedd Branwen.
    Sample B: taken from close to the standing stone at the centre of the mound, which gave 4923 ± 75 B.P. ($\underline{c}$. 2973 B.C.).
    Sample Q: taken from under a stone on the old ground surface, which gave 3353 ± 60 B.P. ($\underline{c}$. 1403 B.C.).
    Sample L: taken from cremated bones, which probably belong to pot B and are consequently associated with a pommel (Corpus no. 13), giving 3257 ± 80 B.P. ($\underline{c}$. 1307 B.C.).
    Sample D: taken from pot L which gave 3224 ± 81 B.P. (1274 B.C.) (B.M. 452).

32. ApSimon 1954, 50.

33. This has been suggested by Taylor 1970, 219. She also suggests that the blade associated with the open-ended pommel (Corpus no. 17) appears similar to ApSimon's Camerton Snowshill group, pointing out that 'one cannot readily differentiate between this (the blade associated with the open-ended pommel) and the Edgington Grave 2, Wilts., dagger', included by ApSimon in his Camerton Snowshill group, appendix C, 58.

34. Evans 1881, 231 (see ref. 11).

35. Thomas 1965-6, 4.

36. Ibid., 4-6.

37. Ibid., 5.

38. Taylor, 1972, 218.

39. Henshall 1968, 183-6.

40. The excavation report is fully published in <u>Archaeologia Cambrensis</u> 126, (1971).

41. Burgess 1962-4, 78-82.

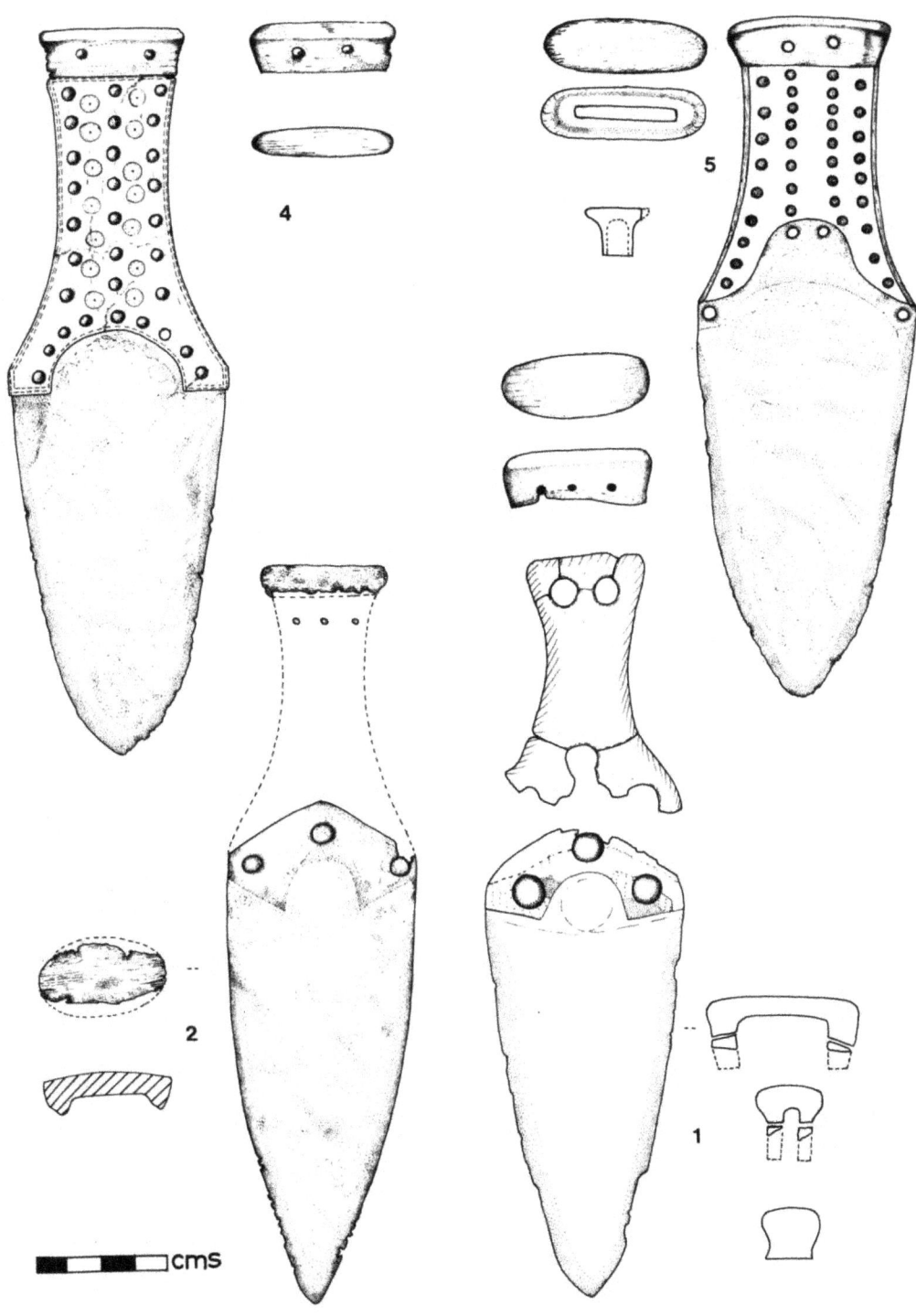

FIG.1. N°1, ASHGROVE, FIFE. (after Henshall). N°2, BARROW 85 AMESBURY, WILTS. N°4, MILSTON GRAVE 51, WILTS. N°5, GARTON SLACK BARROW 107, YORKS.

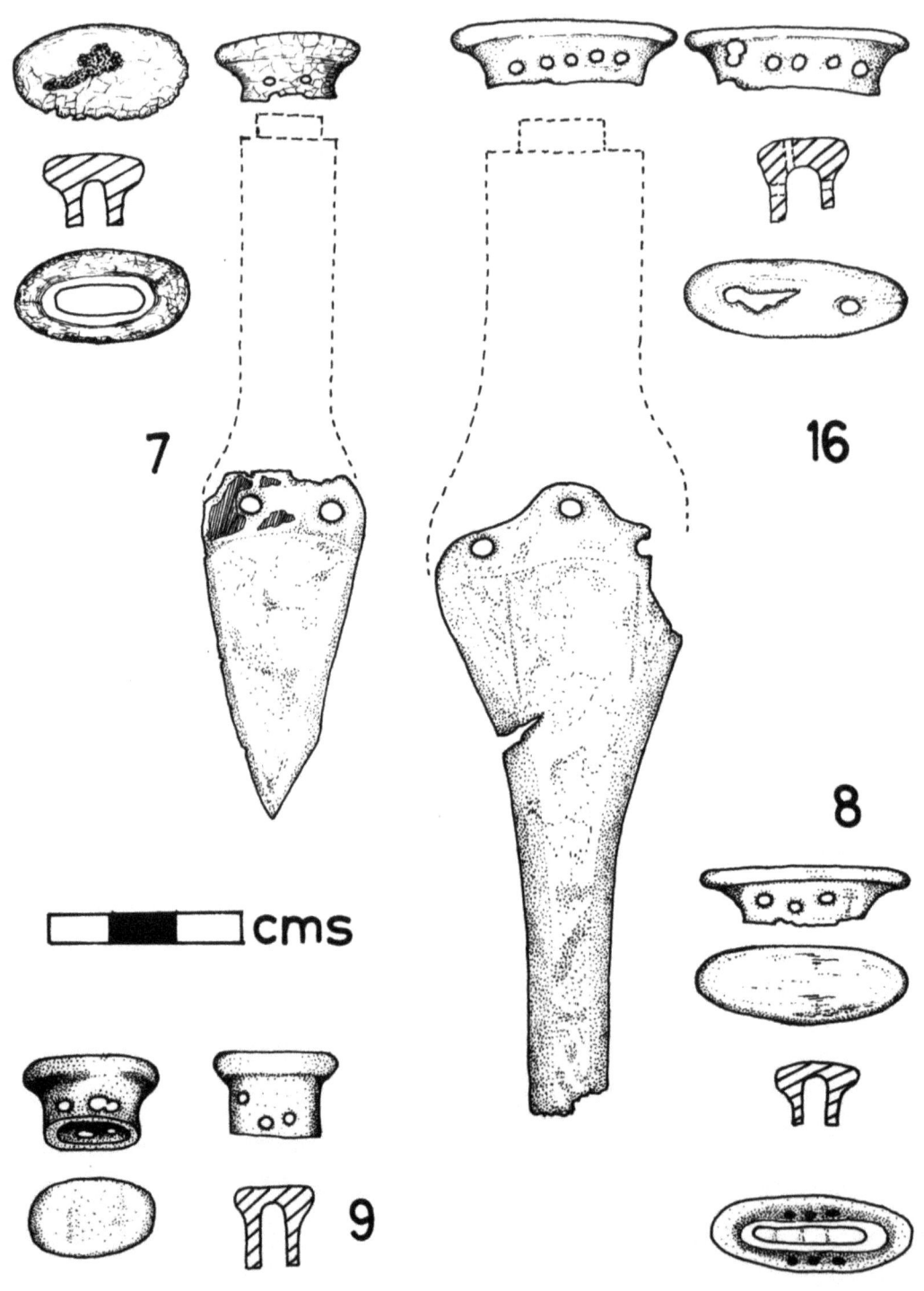

Fig 2. No 7, The MANTON BARROW. No 8, GALLEY LOW. No 9, NARROWDALE HILL. No 16, WINTERBOURNE STOKE G.66.

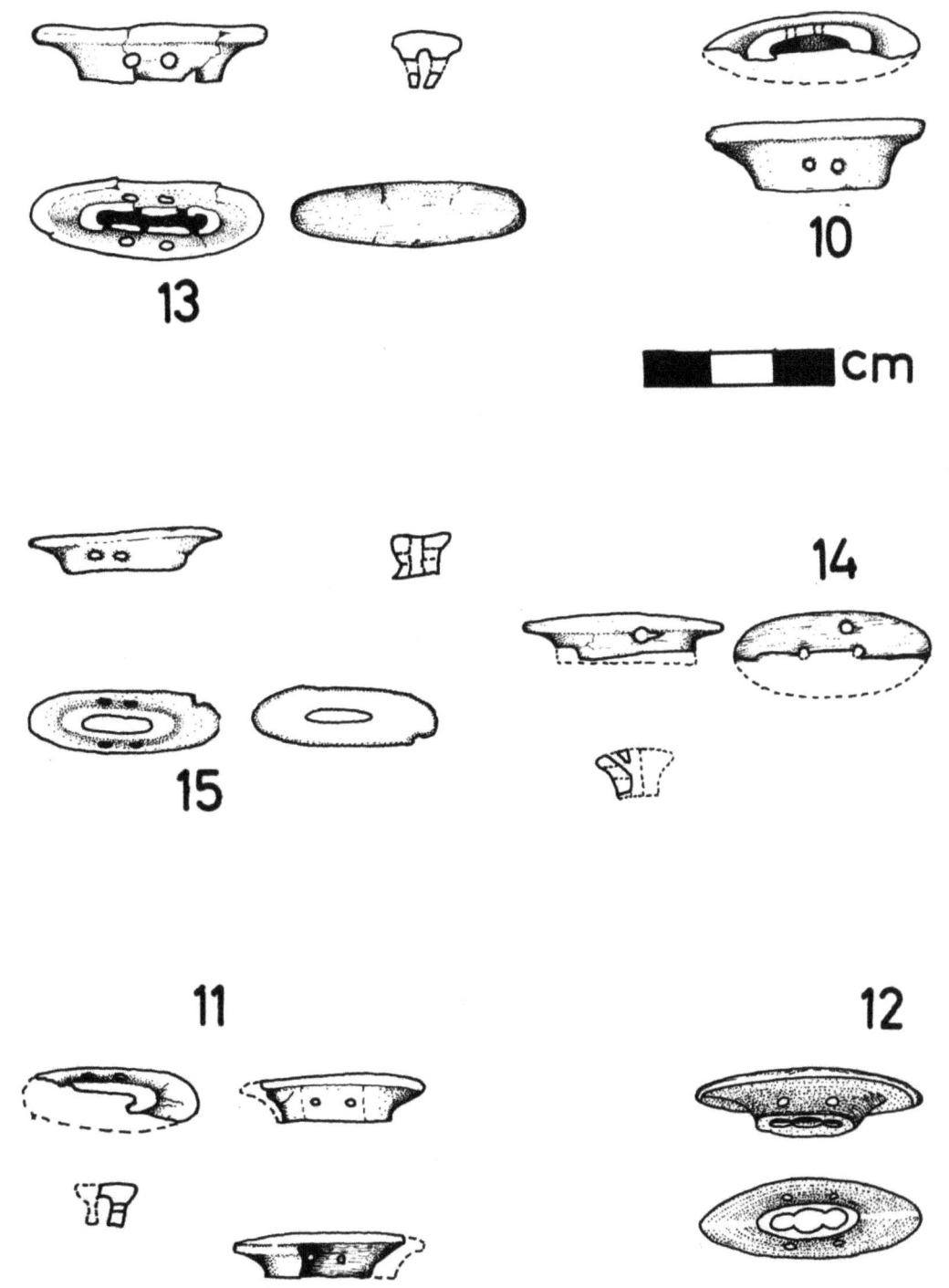

Fig 3. Nº 10, MERDDYN GWYN (after LYNCH). Nº 11, BWYLCH Y RHIW. Nº 12, WILMSLOW (after EVANS). Nº 13 & Nº 14, BEDD BRANWEN. Nº 15, MARIAN BACH.

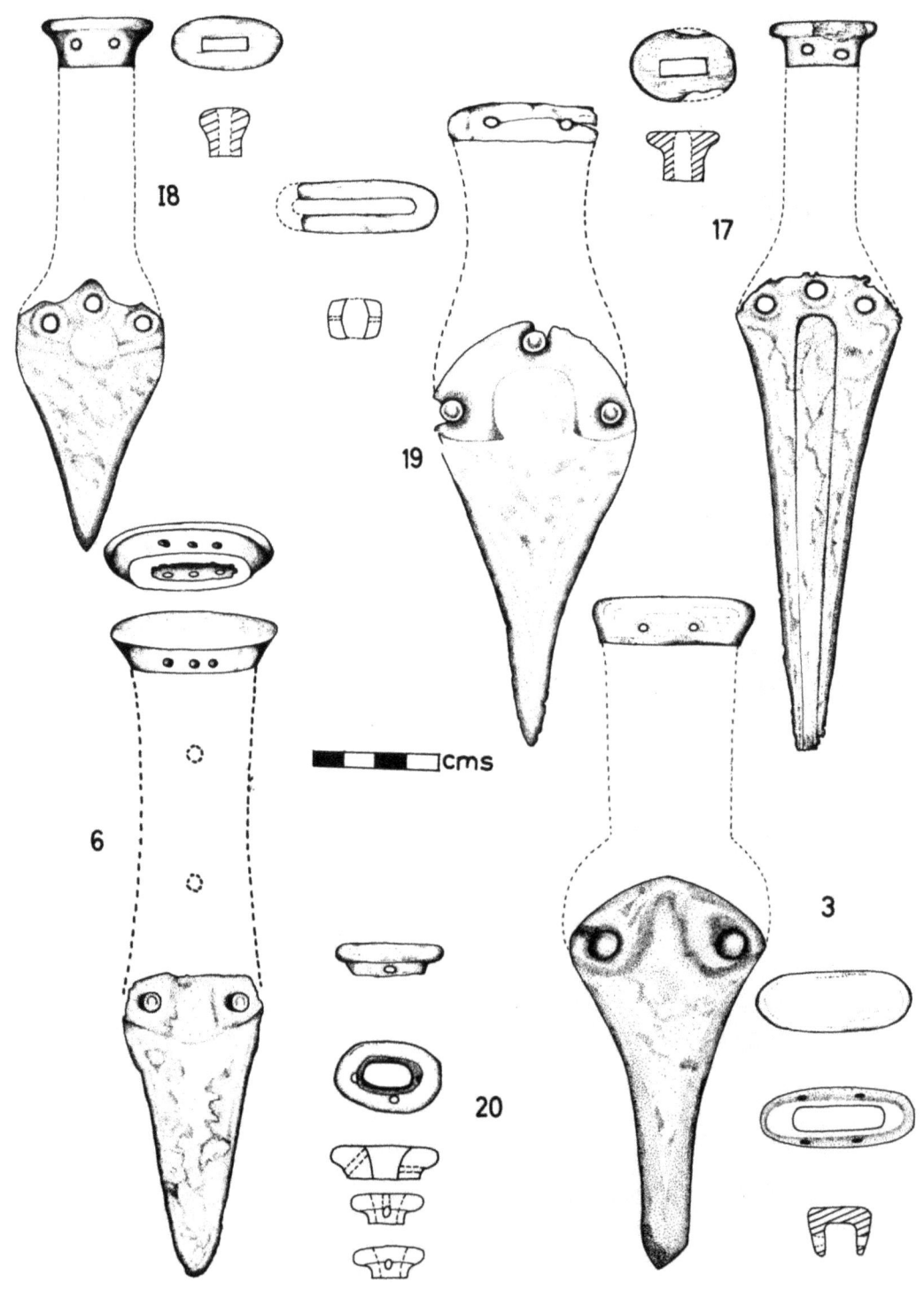

Fig 4. No 3, HELPERTHORPE. No 6, GRISTHORPE. No 17, BARROW 7, THE RIDGEWAY. No 18, EYNSHAM. No 19, GARROWBY WOLD. No 20, STANTON MOOR.

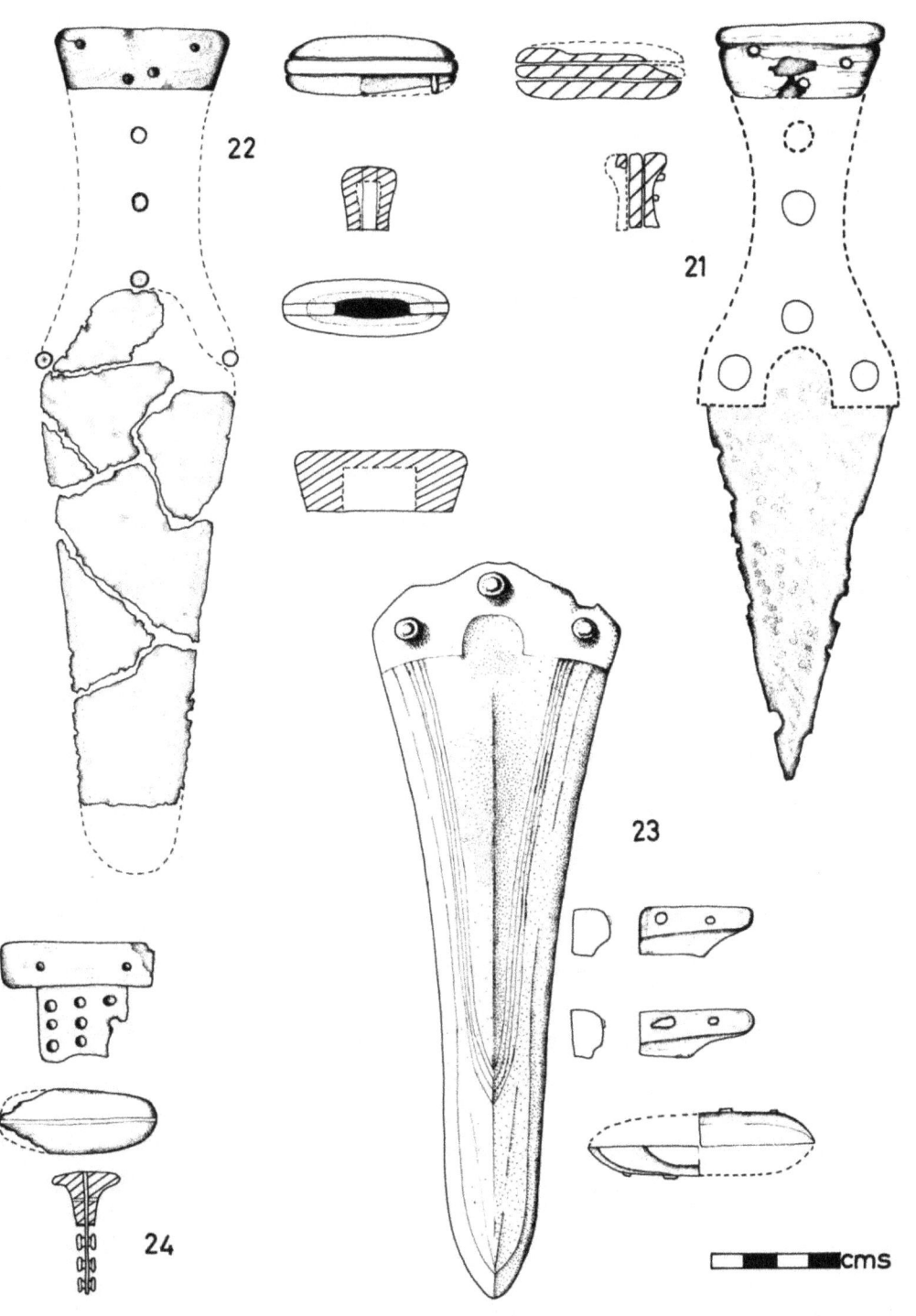

Fig 5. N° 21, LOCKTON WARREN.   N° 22, SCAMRIDGE.

N° 23, WINTERBOURNE STOKE, G 4.   N° 24, LEICESTER.

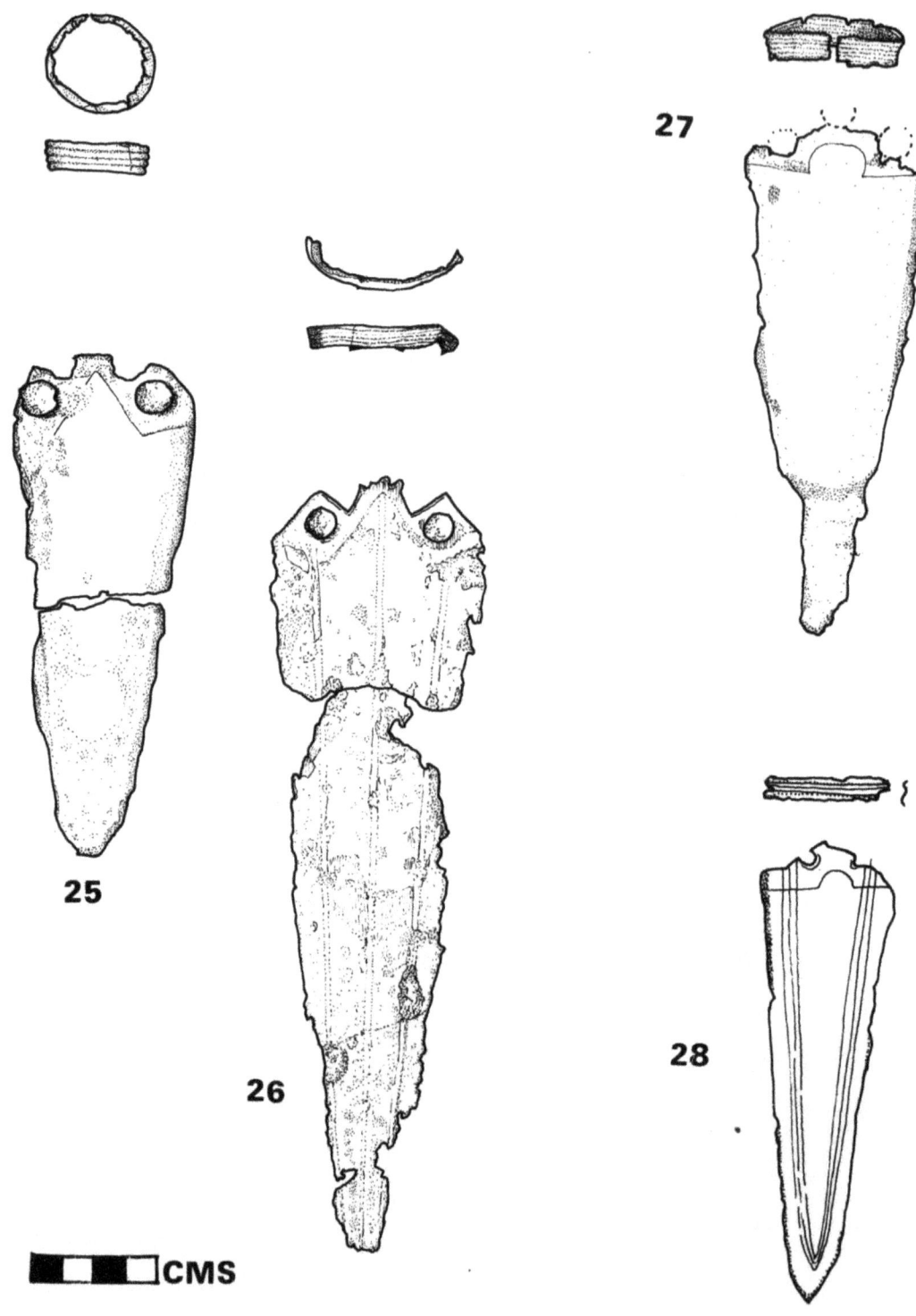

FIG. 6. Nº25, Pommel mount, SKATERAW, EAST LOTHIAN. Nº26, BLACKWATERFOOT, ARRAN. Nº 7, COLLESSIE, FIFE. (all after Henshall); Nº 8, TOPPED MOUNTAIN, CO FERMANAGH.

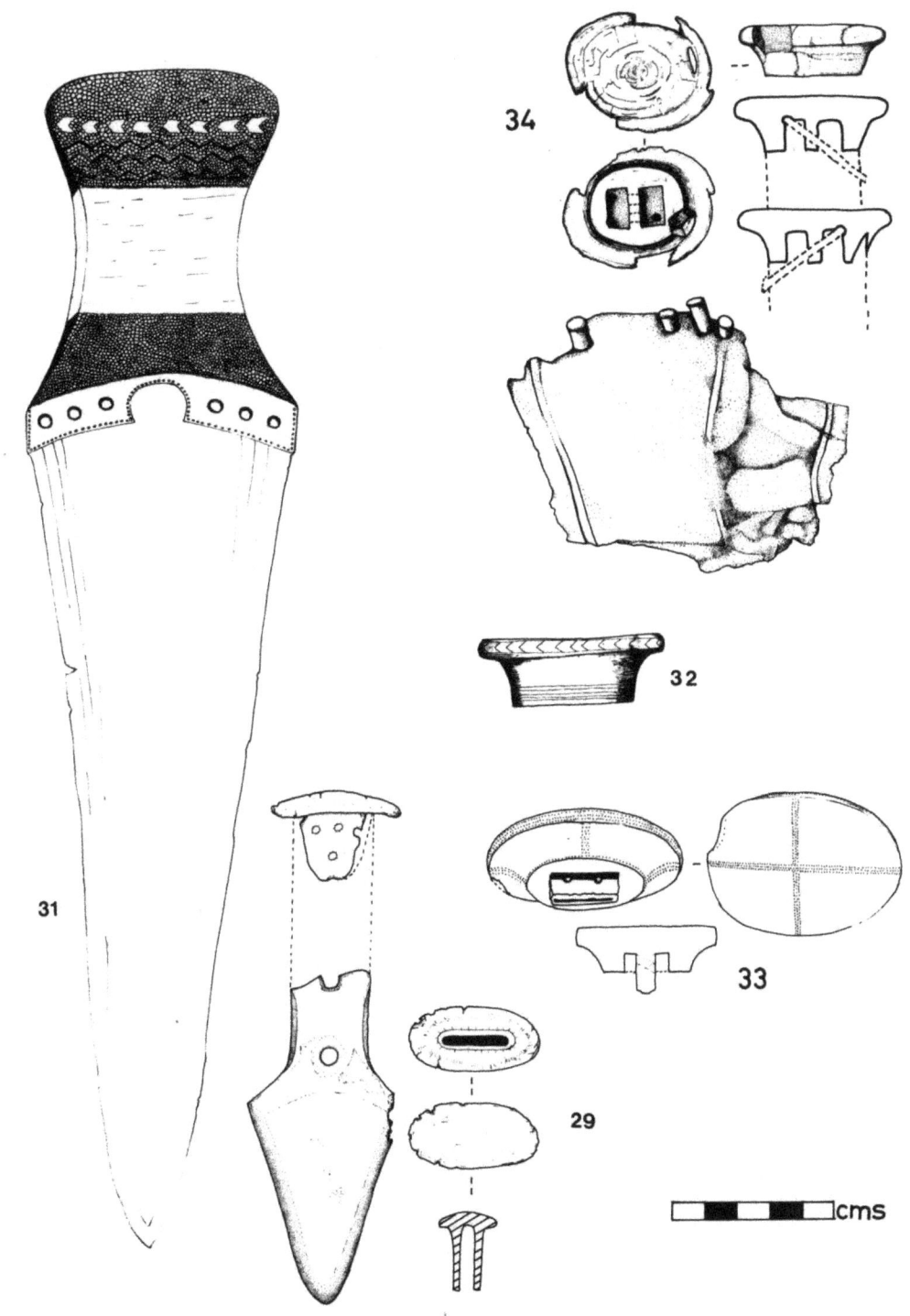

Fig 7. Nº 29, SHREWTON. Nº 31, BUSH BARROW (after Thurnham).

Nº 32, RIDGEWAY GOLD POMMEL. Nº 33, HAMMELDON DOWN (after Evans).

Nº 34, GRANGE.

PLATES Ia and Ib

Gold pommel mount from Topped Mountain, Co. Fermanagh: Corpus no. 28.

Left: exterior view

Right: interior view

(Length approximately 31.5mm.)

(Reproduced by courtesy of the National Museum of Ireland)

PLATES IIa - IIe

Left: Gold pommel from Barrow 7, The Ridgeway, Dorset: Corpus no. 32.

- IIa : Lateral chevron decoration on the side of the pommel cap
- IIb : Neck and underside of the pommel
- IIc : Incised linear decoration on the surface of the pommel cap (scale 1 : 1)
- IId: Lateral view of the collar, showing gold pins in the upper edge.

(Photographs taken by Dr. J.J. Taylor and reproduced with her kind permission).

Right: Amber pommel from Hammeldon Down, Devon: Corpus no. 33.

- IIe : Lateral view, showing pommel tang and pin decoration along the lower surface and upper lip (scale $1 : 2\frac{1}{3}$)

(Reproduced by courtesy of the British Museum)

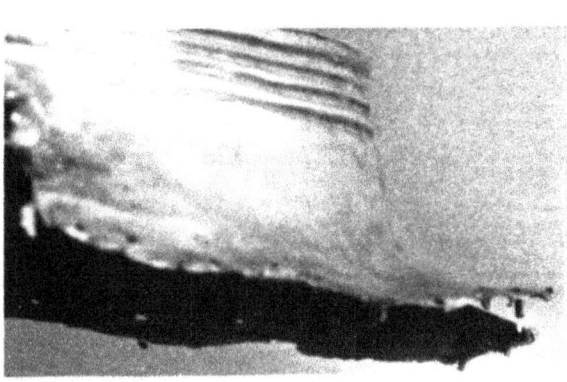